TO TURN A

MILLION

[TTaM]

KEITH ROBINSON.

The information in this book is for general use, and entertainment value. This publication is designed to provide accurate and authoritative information in regard to the subject matter covered. The content is not designed to replace any professional source or services requiring certification or trained personnel. The perspectives shared is not for tax, legal, investment, or career advice and should not be relied on for the purposes of those services. If you have any questions regarding Tax, legal, investment, or career services, individuals are advised to seek advice from their own tax, legal, investment, or career advisors. Please note that neither the information presented nor any opinions expressed in this book is considered confirmation or advisement for ensuing actions and decisions executed by the reader, as they are considered personal in nature. You need to consider your personal situation before taking any actions.

Executive Editor: Harry Claude B.

DEDICATION

To my wife, **Jada L. Robinson**, daughter, **Kayla L. Robinson**, and son, **Jase L. Robinson.**

I dedicate this composition to you with love.

This publication of concepts is for you and those who you bring into this world.

Godspeed!!!

ACKNOWLEDGMENTS

To my mother and father, **Levi** and **Mary Robinson**. Thanks for teaching us that all things are possible if you just believe.

Evelyne, Barbara, Robert, Brett, Norma, Stephanie, Denise, Tracy, Terri, Stephond, and Dana. Thank you for guiding my path for so many years.

A special thank you to my extended family **Velma**, Tammie, Gerald, Kevin, & Misty Jones.

To the CEOs, Presidents, and Chief Procurement Officers who mentored me during my career, Thank you, Thank you, Thank you. The development made a difference.

And special thanks to you, Jimmy Lee Tilman II!!!! The conversation during gym class was just the beginning.

FOREWORD

TO TURN A MILLION

I have had the immense pleasure of knowing Keith Robinson for over 15 years. I can tell that from the moment you are in his presence, greatness exudes. Keith is one of the top executives in the country for process improvement and thought leadership. Based on his life experiences, military background, corporate executive learnings and starting his own financial empowerment research, Keith is a self-taught financial wizard.

So why should you care about reading this book? Well, I will tell you from personal experience that the principles and best practices that you will learn about, will set the tone and foundation for you and your family for a lifetime.

To Turn a Million is an innovative approach to identifying aspirational goals and provides a framework for committing to those goals. All too often we look to our future without thoughtfully planning for it.

If your ambitions are short-term, long-term or recovery, this commonsense approach provides the guidance needed to capture and execute each one of them.

If you like winning, this book gives you and me the playbook to do just that – Win!

Sean M. Suggs,

President,

Toyota, North Carolina.

TABLE OF CONTENTS

DEDICATION												V

ACKNOWLEDGMENTS										VII

FOREWORD												IX

CHAPTER 1

INTRODUCTION											*15*

CHAPTER 2

THINK NEXT STEP										*27*

CHAPTER 3

THE PRINCIPLES OF "TO TURN A MILLION"					*50*

(TTAM)

CHAPTER 4

TTAM WEALTH PLANNING MODEL							*63*

CHAPTER 5

WHY TTAM?											*82*

CHAPTER 6

COMMIT TO YOUR GOAL									*96*

CHAPTER 7

BUILDING WEALTH										*115*

CHAPTER 8

DIVERSIFY WEALTH										*144*

CHAPTER 9

    WEALTH PRESERVATION   *169*

CHAPTER 10

    THE CONCLUSION   *198*

APPENDIX   **217**

CHAPTER 1

INTRODUCTION

If I can take a dollar, multiply it a million times, and then teach you how I did it, would you be interested in learning my approach?????

This is a question I have asked my children over the course of their development years to grab their attention. Perhaps this question would be enough for me to grab your attention as well; I certainly hope it is, and if it is so...

Let's take a moment to do a sanity check. Are you someone who is interested in learning concepts about building wealth? If you are, let me take you forward and further into the journey of this manifesto. Before we begin, I want you to know that you will need to confront your fears. Those very things have, for so very long, managed to hold you back.

Naturally, you may have questions about building wealth. There are quite a few times when we find ourselves thinking out loud, often asking the people around us for answers to the questions that have long been unanswered. At times, very few people have answers that actually make sense. If you agree with me, then I believe that your situation is not very different than the situation I found myself in at the start of my journey. So, how about we start at the beginning of that journey?

In the early years of my life, I remember seeing people driving exotic cars and fancy boats, and all I could do, as a young man who knew rather less at the time, was wonder how they were able to afford it. "How can a person manage to get to that level of wealth?" This was one of the many times in my life I was cognizant of those people who I would put in the category of "Haves" while I would place myself in the category of "Have Nots." You may be able to relate to my situation.

I later realized that the question I was asking had more to do with a person's financial situation, and in another respect, the question had something to do with my state of mind. To wonder why there are people who have assets that others only ever dream of is a question you will get from someone who is looking for the road to a higher level of wealth. Especially if the question is coming from someone serious about taking a wealth-building journey.

The starting line for that journey begins with the second question, "What can a person do to be in the category of the "Haves" versus the "Have Nots?" To tell you the truth, it is the very question that I asked myself, the question that ignited a spark in me that generated a flame big enough to get me to where I had wanted to be. And more importantly, it is the same question that this book aims to answer. Additionally, this book aims to share with you the same approach I took that made me one of the "Haves." And hopefully pass on a similar spark that could ignite your inspiration as well.

As we embark on the journey through this publication, a philosophy of sorts, we are going to look at quite a few aspects of planning that can guide our path and explore how those aspects center around opportunities that affords us a chance for growth and wealth development.

Some of the concepts I will share may be new to you. To help you through the content, I am committed to taking a commonsense approach and handling important factors responsibly. It is important to note that building wealth takes time. It typically doesn't happen overnight and is a result of short-term and long-term planning. We all know the old adage about fast money – "It's easy come and easy go." Wealth is sustainable if you plan for it in a way that results in long-term sustainability.

Our journey will start with a foundation that examines the current state of wealth. We will then pivot to concepts that help with building a wealth plan. Ultimately, the goal of this book is to help you establish a personally developed wealth-building plan for your future stated goals. We will give some consideration to how wealth is built through income and investing. As we give consideration to wealth-building options, we will not take the approach that one avenue is better than the other, for these decisions are personal in nature. However, we will discuss available avenues that provide the ability to put money to work in an effort to support the achievement of your personal wealth plan and future goals.

If any of this frightens you, please go back to the third paragraph and revisit the sanity check. You will need to overcome your fears. You may not recognize the fears lurking inside that I am referring to. They are the negative perceptions often hiding behind the thoughts we think or the things we tell ourselves. Those negativities are messages we speak from within that convey "you can't have wealth", "a better home", "a more reliable car", or "a better income stream." The more you tell yourself these things, the more you defeat your dreams and rob yourself of something potentially greater. In the end, you will settle for the mundane, and the longer it last, atrophy will set in on your ability to dream, thus making it even harder to build toward future success.

Your views about your future are quite important, and they will help decide your destiny in part. After all, your ideas influence your behaviors, which in turn influence your results. When you listen to your fears, in this context, you are allowing them to achieve their aim of dragging you down and preventing you from surpassing their achievement. Oftentimes we are afraid of failing. We don't think we have the ability to accomplish a desired goal.

Is this something you struggle with? Do you think you are not good enough? If you do, I know how you feel. I've felt that way myself at times. But here's the thing: fear is normal, and it is quite natural. Overcoming fear is also a normal and natural thing to do. In order to build wealth, one must overcome their fears.

What is the worst that can happen if you decide to overcome your fears by deciding to develop a plan that aligns with your dreams and aspirational goals? We typically found that the things we worried about rarely happen. Our concerns in life are not always as horrible as we imagine. Generally, we are resilient, and typically overcome any major hurdles we are faced with. When we fall, we get right back up. It is as simple as that.

Getting rid of the fears is the foremost thing in this process that you have to tackle. This can be done by finding a burning platform that is important and self-motivating to you. Significant growth generally happens when a person finds a compelling reason to grow beyond their current situation. So, let's take a brief moment to allow you to find the core reason for your "Why."

You can start by asking yourself, ""Why" does building wealth matter to me?" If the answer comes to you immediately, I want you to embrace it. Allow the answer to become something you cleave to during your pursuit of building wealth. I want you to reflect on your burning platform from time to time. It may be considered "the spark that ignites your fire." If you remove your fears and establish your motivation, before you know it, you will be on your personal journey to become one of the "Have."

Conquering fear and achieving a life goal can be a daunting task – overwhelming and intimidating. Just by taking one small step forward, sometimes that is all it takes to build your confidence. After that achievement, you may build momentum by doing it again, and before you know it, those modest steps will allow you to achieve a mountain of success. It's the same for life as it is for building and maintaining wealth.

The point of this whole exercise is that you must first believe you can become wealthy. You see, even someone with low wages can become wealthy if they are disciplined with their savings, moderate with their expenditures, and stick with it for a long period of time. It is not beyond the horizon of possibilities if you overcome your fears and take the initiative.

You must own your success, by working to achieve it. How you start out in life does not mean you have to finish it out the same way. Your pace of earnings, whether slow or fast, can be improved. Just because you have not been able to save much, does not mean you have to keep up with the same pattern of living. These are the types of concepts that we will thoroughly discuss, things that are hindrances to your path toward financial independence and stability.

Before moving forward, I will tell you that, like any other form of success, becoming wealthy is not going to be an overnight process. It will be the result of proper planning and commitment;

This will be achieved through building a plan and working the plan you build. In all honesty, it's going to take time. Remember that investing in yourself is a long-term commitment.

If you follow me on this journey and hold all I say nearer to your heart, you will be well on your way to securing a plan for your financial future. While the journey will be lengthy and the path may not always be simple, remember your "Why." It will be the burning platform that inspires your commitment and success.

Now, with all that being said, let's get started, shall we?

CHAPTER 2

THINK NEXT STEP

Success is an accumulation of steps executed in accordance with a mission or vision. Steps can be forward, lateral, or backwards depending on what is required for advancement. Fundamentally, when we set goals, it is incumbent of us to "Think Next Step."

Thinking next step requires a progressive mindset, to develop it, start by asking: where am I currently, where do I want to be, and how long will it take to get there. It doesn't matter if you are starting a business, looking for a new job, or adopting excellent habits, this way of thinking is critical to move forward, and moving forward requires a game plan that needs a good offense.

Have you ever heard the phrase "the best defense is a good offense?" This phrase has been used in a variety of circumstances, and is most known as a strategy for war. We use it here as a reminder of the journey we are charting, and also remind us to turn stumbling blocks into stepping stones. A solid offensive for us begins with knowing where we are, and planning where we want to go. Our strong defense is how we carry out the strategy while being completely prepared to do so. There are a few factors taken into account during implementation. First, we must decide on a course of action. Second, we must proceed with caution. Third, we must consider risk as we execute. Wealth creation does not occur without the implementation of a well-established and executed strategy.

For a strategy to be considered well established, it will need to have a primary aim, or goal. As an example, your strategic aim or goal must align with where you want to go and where you ultimately want to be. Let's say you want to have a specific income; your strategy will need to confirm that the income is possible once the strategy is executed. Therefore, you are not going to make a strategy unless it will assist you in accomplishing the long-term objectives. This is core to thinking next step. It is part of understanding where you currently are and everything that led you to this place. Your previous strategy played a role in where you are currently. Setting clear goals to achieve, a vision to achieve it, and having the motivation to execute the plan is what helps a person obtain their aspirations.

(1)   Take a moment to reflect directionally on where you want to be? Also, reflect on when you want to get there.

At this point, it is good to reflect on your source of motivation. "Your Why." Having a goal is just part of the equation. Finding the motivation is the other part. So, what's motivating you now, and what will keep you motivated while executing your plans? Is it the pursuit of wealth? Is it the pursuit of prosperity? Or is it simply having the presence of mind to shift from your current situation and onto a path of potentially greater success?

In discovering the answer to these questions, if you really think about it, you have already started thinking next step. Leverage this thinking to ignite your process. The process starts with defining a direction, and it should be forward, and leading you to a path that takes you to the success you seek. Remember to consider that it will take some time to get there. Nothing about success is overnight, but then again, the longer the journey, the sweeter the destination feels. It's almost like having a dream that became reality.

Everyone who has ever made an impact on the world had a dream. Whether they founded a company, ruled a nation, or launched a movement, it all began in their head and hearts as a dream. Initially, the fantasy may have been loaded with aspirations of fame, money, or power. They may have imagined success, acclaim, or respect. Eventually, they achieved their goals, and probably through a well-executed strategy.

You may have fantasized about things you've wanted in life. Some of them may be in your possession, while others may not. However, we have heard people say that nothing is impossible; let's put it to the test as we build and execute the wealth plan that helps to obtain the things we want out of life. We know that striving to accomplish your goals is more essential than simply fantasizing about them. Properly planning will allow for personal accountability and enable the discipline needed to achieve the goals.

What is your fate? Where do you see yourself in five years? Or how about ten years from now... or thirty? Of course, no one can answer that question with assurance, no matter how hard we try. But, while we cannot foresee our fate, we can certainly know and modify our course. The path to one's destiny is always marked by the urge to get there. Motivation is a factor that prevents you from giving up too soon. Your thoughts, plans, and roadmaps are the pathway to your destiny. Without these, you risk getting off track – or worse, going nowhere.

When we make decisions, results are often immediate. However, there are times when the impact of our decisions is not realized until much later. If the decision, for example, was done without planning, and there was no immediate growth resulting from it, you may get discouraged, and left with a pattern of "I need to figure it out." Fundamentally, "thinking next step" would've inspired you to develop a roadmap, which would have provided a deeper perspective on when the results of the decision will be manifested.

This way of thinking is definitely like exercising a muscle. The technique requires us to shift our mindset in order to correctly execute a course of action. Having the mindset to think next step, has more to do with establishing direction. When you have a direction of focus, you can effectively plan the course of action required to make the destination a reality.

Direction setting is very important. Everyone should be mindful of their current situation in life. Whether the current situation is good or bad, moving forward shouldn't be left to chance. You can take ownership of your life by knowing where you are and where you want to go. Implicitly, there should be a gap. In order to close the gap to your destination, a bridge between the current situation and destination is built. The bridge will be a straight-line pathway in the direction you are heading. An important aspect to remember is that everyone's bridge from current to future state is different, and customized to the direction they define and the gap they are trying to close. The bridge defines the steps needed to get to your destination. It is important to take those steps with good measure and in a calculated manner.

(2) Take a moment to reflect on what steps are needed for your plan? The template below is a good tool to use for capturing the steps and timing:

Think Next Step Template			
Plan (What actions do you want to achieve)	**Timing** (When do you want to achieve it)	**Risk to Mitigate** (What challenges are in The Way)	**Actions** (What actions will overcome challenges)

By leveraging the template above, it is possible to layout the following:

1. The directional steps required for the plan
2. The timing for when the step needs to be executed
3. The potential risk that can impact execution
4. The mitigation that provides the ability to overcome risk factors.

Now that we've reviewed what it takes to have direction, let's delve into the manner of taking calculated steps. Calculated steps can be described as "steps" taken after considerable thought has been given. If you are mindful of benefits and impediments before proceeding with any forward planning, in some aspect, calculated steps were considered. Calculated steps are critical to every element of your journey. One of the main purposes for thinking next step is that risks and concerns are taking into consideration.

There are numerous ways of approaching this technique. Some of the common methods include comparing plus and minus factors associated with the direction you want to take. The following template is a good framework for constructing plus and minus factors associated with any decisions being planned. By doing this, you gain a sense of the challenges you must overcome and the benefits of moving forward. If the challenges are too great, you have to rethink the plan or come up with contingencies.

Decision Template		
Plan (What actions do you want to take)	Plus (+) Benefit of taking the action	Minus (-) Negative Impact of taking the action

Another way of approaching this aspect of thinking next step is through benefit analysis. The benefit analysis approach gives you the ability to look at factors in a different way. With benefit analysis, you layout factors on a matrix that helps you hone in on a decision. For example, let's say you need to consider the benefit you will get from the effort that's required to achieve results. The benefit analysis is a good way of visualizing the decision you are making. In this example, if the benefit is low and the effort is high, you may choose another path forward. Conversely, if the benefit outweighs the effort, you may consider moving forward with your plan. There may be other factors to consider as well, and using this approach can help with identifying them.

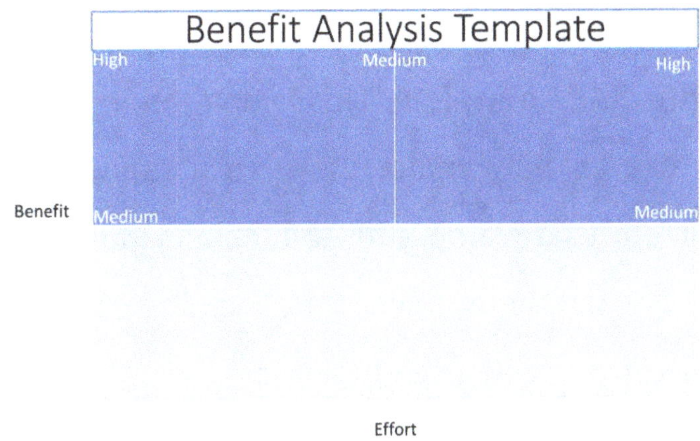

Here are a few more factors you may consider charting on your matrix: Benefit vs. Cost, Benefit vs. Time Required, and Benefit vs. Resources. Depending on the factors, the benefit analysis matrix will help visualize and prioritize them. This approach also helps bring awareness to risks that may exist within the factors being weighed. Risk should be fully understood so that it is mitigated as you move forward with your plans.

The next step is to determine when you want to achieve those incremental progression identified on your plan. This is defined in terms of years. To help make the plan a reality, it's important to develop additional skills along the way. This will boost the value of core competencies you already possess.

As an example, a professor with a Master's degree, can only earn a certain amount of salary, but if they have a Ph.D. and tenure, earning potential could be significantly more. If you start with a bachelor's degree but incrementally increase your value by learning a foreign language, obtaining advanced degrees, certifications, or earning a Ph.D., you are also making a proposition for incremental values and income potential. When you decide a path for the things you want to pursue, the things that will reinforce talents you already have, you are determining the steps that will bring you incremental success. For instance, if someone is just finishing school, or starting a new career, they have to decide the next goal and by when they are planning to achieve the goal. This will form the bases of their strategy. Thinking next step allows you to have the foresight needed to gradually and thoughtfully build a plan and work your way through it. You will undoubtedly have to consider the time period and effort that it may demand. Specify the length of time needed for the voyage. A personal development plan template can help capture your ideas.

Personal Development Plans Template	
Personal Development (Create a list of personal development goals)	**Timing** (By when will this be completed)

If you are thinking about it in the context of a business, the next step may be to start one. You may want to begin in your home, by gradually executing a growth strategy that will ultimately allow you to scale up, and eventually be able to move into your own office complex, where you may have the possibility to see or reach more people. Then, perhaps, over time, you want to develop it to a much bigger scope of business, in terms of revenue or even globally.

Over time, you will gain the experience needed for growth. However, you need to specify the stages aligning to the goals you must complete in order to get the incremental advantages. It is the same as declaring, "I know where I want to go." And only by saying that, the stage of personal or professional development begins. The following step is "I know what I have to do," followed by "This is my timeframe."

Understand your foreseeable Risks.

A plan should not proceed without taking a risk-based approach. We can define a risk-based approach as one that allows you to identify the risk prior to the presents or impact it may have. Risk factors play an important role when thinking next step and are equally as important to the other components of next step thinking previously discussed. Having a good understanding of risk factors from a fundamental level means that you have a grasp of your forward planning and understand it well enough to provide judgment into the plan's vulnerable elements. The vulnerable areas of a plan can challenge and derail advancement as a plan moves forward.

There are ways to address risk. You can first find where it's lurking, confirm if it is real, consider the impact it could have, and then address it. If you can do these things, you will be better positioned to visualize risk and mitigate it.

Identifying and addressing risk is essential to any plan, and it should not be done in a vacuum. Letting others provide their point of view on risk may be needed. Input from others may provide risk factors that the person developing the plan may not have considered.

Even if the person who created the plan cannot see the same risk factors, they should still give allowance to the outsider's perspective. Allow other viewpoints, not for the derailment of the plan, but to mitigate risk and develop a path forward that has less risk. Ultimately, the purpose is to be successful in achieving the goals.

Identifying risk can invoke fear

Growth can only occur when you have the fortitude to push yourself outside your comfort zone. Bravery and fear coexist, but most people are unwilling to accept them.

The reality, though, is what Mark Twain says about bravery and fear. "When we have bravery, we can stand up to our fears." However, this resistance does not eliminate all of our anxiety. Even the bravest person has something to be afraid of. The capacity to take risks by being brave enough to step outside of your comfort zone is what's important. Fear frequently occurs when it is time to take the initial step. In actuality, staying in our comfort zone is more about apprehension than it is about the ability to execute.

To attain your objectives, you must first be brave enough to break through the bond fear has on you. Through bravery, you can get to the source of the fear and overcome it. A brave person may manage to defeat their fear by understanding the triggers that evoke fear, and develop effective coping skills or mechanisms to significantly reduce or eliminate the fear. That is why we think next step and take a risk-based approach to achieving our strategy, which is a process that is more targeted and straightforward in nature. The approach we will discuss provides the ability to take action without moving completely out of our comfort zone.

Let's start understanding our fears by drawing a circle. In the middle of the circle are the things we can control. Outside of the circle are the things we cannot control. Our strategy will be built around the things we can control. We will place those things in the middle of the circle.   We can be less fearful, when the controllable items are within our power of influence. Ultimately, we can take action on the things that are within our control, and comfort in knowing that we are in charge of the destiny associated with them.

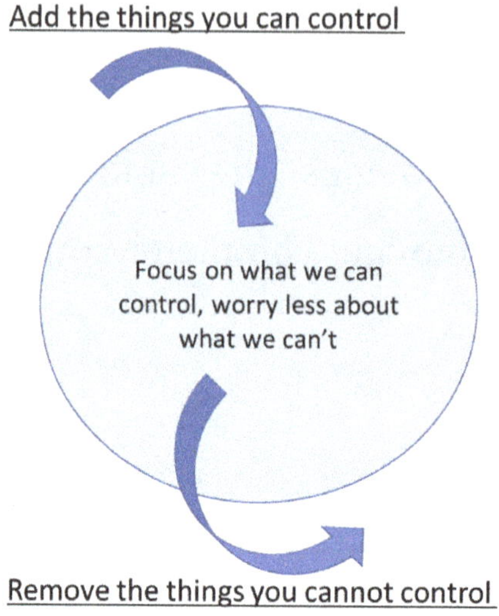

There are other benefits to this approach. Which will arm you with the needed mindset to protect your plan from external factors that might cause you to lose sight of your objectives and goals. Self-doubt should not be allowed to discourage your plan. Hesitancy happens in life and we must confront it. We must resist the impulse of becoming our own worst enemy, and be confident enough to see the plan through. All too often in life, we hold ourselves back due to fear and risk. As a result, we never push ourselves forward. Which is why we will take a risk-based approach, as we increase the possibility of achieving the wealth plan.

To "Think Next Step," you will need to consider three factors; the direction of the plan, take calculated steps, and addressing risk. Without proper consideration of these factors, it's difficult to build a plan that has the structural integrity needed to withstand scrutiny over time.

Now that we have the mindset to "Think Next Step," let's see how this mindset matters to the principles of "To Turn a Million."

CHAPTER 3

THE PRINCIPLES OF "TO TURN A MILLION" (TTaM)

To Turn a Million (TTaM), whenever I speak those words, I always get that look. You know, that quizzical look that's asking the question, "What's That?" Contrary to what may come to mind, and I am sure it varies.

"To Turn a Million" is a term referencing the pace of earnings. The term considers how fast it takes a person to earn a million dollars of income or a company's pace for generating a million dollars of revenue.

There are three main components to the TTaM calculation;

(1)   Income,

(2)   Annual Time, and

(3)   The Constant - $1 Million.

When these factors are pulled together within a model, the output provides a picture of the pace of earnings. For standardization, $1 Million is the constant. It helps bring consistency to the rubric. The portion that varies from person to person or business to business is annual compensation. This is easily understood due to earnings and compensation varying from person to person. Let's take a brief moment to understand how these components are modeled in an equation:

$$\frac{\text{Constant (\$)}}{\text{Annual Income or Revenue (\$)}} = \text{Number of years it takes to earn a million dollars(yr.)}$$

The TTaM equation is not too intimidating. It can be solved by simply taking the constant, $1,000,000, and dividing it by anyone's annual income. For example: let's say a person earns $50,000 a year, their TTaM pace will be 20 years. Essentially, it will take that person 20 years to earn a million dollars at an income of $50,000. The equation below captures the output associated with that person's inputs:

$$\text{TTaM Pace} = \frac{\$1,000,000}{\$50,000 \text{ yearly}} = 20 \text{ years.}$$

Now that you have a perspective on the concept and how the math works, this is a good place to give consideration to your TTaM Pace.

Simply divide into $1,000,000 your annual income or revenue to determine your pace of earnings. The output is your TTaM pace. You should write the value down. The number you came up with is a baseline of your current pace of earning, and the value may cause you to "Think Next Step." However, at this point, there is no judgment regarding how good or bad your pace may be. We should spend some time characterizing what the number may indicate, which is certainly not carved in stone; but varies as income increases or decreases.

When it comes to building wealth, you want your baseline TTaM number to decrease over time. The smaller the number, the better. This perspective can be represented by an example of a person who is earning $20,000 per year; their TTaM pace is 50. Similarly, a person making $200,000 per year, their TTaM pace will be 5. By perception, the person with a 5-year pace could be in a position to build wealth faster than the person with a TTaM pace of 50. The person with the 5-year pace must be financially responsible with their earnings. If someone has a significant amount of expenses and a fair amount of debt, they will find it challenging to build wealth. On the other hand, a person with a TTaM pace of 50 will be able to build wealth if they are able to keep their expenses down while maintaining a low debt structure. We will discuss both of these points in subsequent chapters.

The pace of earnings is vital to building wealth. When you reflect on the principles of TTaM, you realize that this is one of the driving forces behind why we pursue income or revenue growth. By doing so, we are accelerating our pace of earning and thus putting ourselves in a better position to generate wealth. Just like someone driving a car will typically accelerate to their destination, they will be in a position to get there faster.

When I reflect on my youth, I realize that my parents had difficulty accelerating their earnings pace. When I was younger, I was always conscientious of what we could afford, and fully aware of my parent's financial limitations. During that period, I could clearly see the household funds depleting before the end of the month. The next paycheck couldn't come fast enough, as bills and personal needs were waiting for it.

Wealth was modest in my household. I wouldn't go as far as saying that we were poor, but we definitely were not buying exotic cars or boats, and our home size was relatively modest.

My parents were like most other parents who wanted the most for their children, and they were willing to do all they could for us. There was a lot of emphasis on the things that would help us see a better future, one that would require us to keep moving forward in life. It is probably one of the reasons I developed "keep moving forward" as my personal mantra. Throughout my journey, this mantra was used to motivate me as I was thinking of my next steps in life.

There were some personal decisions being made along the way. The best decision started with understanding the things successful people had done and then following that journey. By growing up in a home with parents and siblings who constantly believed in one another, I definitely had the confidence needed to pursue a path like that. Honestly, that path was more about building a future for myself and one that would foster some level of wealth.

For me to get there, I needed to have a plan and the discipline to follow it. Once I began to understand how money works, I eventually learned that my incremental growth in income was creating a faster pace of earnings, and that pace is known as "To Turn a Million," and accelerating that pace became my goal.

Over the course of my life, I met people of all levels of success. Some of those people had a TTaM pace of 1 or less. I have also met folks who had a TTaM pace of 50 or more. For the purpose of our journey through this manifesto, we are not defining what makes a person successful but to leverage this approach, at a foundational level, for planning how to build wealth. It is also important that we don't minimize the influence a person's pace of earning will have on their ability to build wealth. It is only rational that we understand that making money faster than you are spending it, puts you in a more advantageous position for building wealth. Therefore, your plan must be consistent with the above mentioned.

Let's take a moment to reflect on people who have a TTaM pace of 1 or less. One of my astute observations about them is that they did not allow themselves to become stagnant, and at some point, they had a plan for what they wanted to accomplish. Some of these folks had exponential growth while executing their plan. If there were skills they needed, they obtained them. If there were career changes they needed to make, they made them. If they were interacting with toxic people and needed to move away from them, they moved away from them. If they knew the things that were holding them back from reaching their potential, they got rid of them. After getting their freight train on the tracks, and moving in the direction they desired to go, there was nothing that was going to stop them from achieving the train's time schedule, and it was fascinating watching them navigate their journey, like it was "full steam ahead." Let's keep their fortitude in mind so that it serves as a source of motivation, and inspires in us the perspective of; "If they can do it, I can too."

There are some paradigms you may need to shift as you navigate your course. We are always taught to follow our passion and do what we like to do. However, doing what we like to do can be the crutch that prevents us from stepping out of our comfort zone, and we may need to step out of our comfort zone, from time to time, in order to build wealth.

My message here is that it is ok to do what you like, especially if it gets you the TTaM pace you desire, but the other consideration is who you are doing it with. Just think about it, we all have engaged in activities that resulted in us having the best times of our lives, and it was an endeavor we truly liked. But, if you reflect on it, the people we were doing it with also contributed to how much we enjoyed it.

Now, let's reflect on the same activity, but change the people we like with people we don't.

We will probably find ourselves being miserable while doing the very things we love.

For illustration purposes, let's say you like playing a sport. When you play it with your friends, you have all the fun in the world. Now imagine playing the sport with someone you just don't want to be around. You probably can't wait for the games to be over.

As you build and execute your TTaM plan, you may find yourself working with people you don't align with. Know that the moment is temporary. Your plan will be forecasting your next steps, and you will also be building the necessary skills that will prevent you from becoming stagnant. Those skills will be leveraged to keep you moving forward.

This chapter provided more depth into the philosophy of To Turn a Million. The fundamental principle is a metric that measures the pace of earnings, and that pace, as you increase it, will help put you into a position to generate wealth. Of course, the pace of earning is just one part of it; building a plan to get there is the other part.

Now that we have this understanding, let's explore TTaM's wealth planning model.

CHAPTER 4

TTaM WEALTH PLANNING MODEL

The pace of earnings is an informative way to judge your ability to build wealth. This is where we start with TTaM. At this point, you can ask yourself, "How do you improve the TTaM pace?" We will answer that question in this chapter. Additionally, we will introduce each element of the model and their importance.

We start with the TTaM calculation to gain a picture of the current state of earnings. However, other elements within the model bring together a holistic approach to TTaM. This approach is known as the TTaM Wealth Planning Model. The model serves as a forward-looking guide that can be leveraged to build a plan for the future state of wealth. There are 4 primary elements to the TTaM model:

1. The TTaM paceline,
2. The goals you aim to achieve,
3. The timing for achieving your goals, and
4. The personal development plan.

1. The TTaM Paceline

You currently understand TTaM Pace as it relates to earnings and revenue. When we described it previously, it was for the current state of income. At that time, there was no judgment as to what it meant concerning your current situation. But, as we go forward, we need to think of it with respect to building your future plan; we now have to consider the gap that exists between where you are and where you want to be. This is the point where judgment is made. Let's take a moment to consider your current pace of earnings. This will be the number you calculated in Chapter 3. For a quick refresher, you simply divide $1,000,000 by your annual income or revenue. Reference the formula below:

$$\frac{\text{Constant (\$)}}{\text{Annual Income or Revenue (\$)}} = \text{Number of years it takes to earn a million dollars(yr.)}$$

As an example, if you earn $50,000 annually, it will take 20 years To Turn a Million.

$$\text{TTaM Pace} = \frac{\$1,000,000}{\$50,000 \text{ yearly}} = 20 \text{ years.}$$

The example above results in a whole number (no decimal). When TTaM pace is calculated for your actual salary, you may get a number that has a decimal. The numbers following the decimal are the months associated with the pace, while the number in front of the decimal represents the number of years it will take "To Turn a Million."

By now, you should have a picture of your current state. The question you want to answer now is, What TTaM pace do you want to have 10 years from now? This answer will vary from person to person or business to business. No response is right or wrong. The answer is specific to the person building their personal wealth plan.

I like to use 10 years for a forward-looking point of view. To me, looking 10 years into the future is far enough away for planning but close enough to connect to present-day trends.

Generally, we create reference points in association with decades. Our memories contain accounts of what we were doing in our twenties, thirties, forties, and fifties, which reflect decades of experience and learning. No matter where you are in your journey, the next 10 years matter. A 10-year time frame also allows for enough continuity for a long-range vision for wealth planning and building. 10 years from now will be a good reference point for how well you executed your plan.

Let's look at this in the context of the equation below. In this example, we currently have a 20-year TTaM pace. Our aspirational goal is to have a 10-year TTaM pace. Keep in mind that the lower number reflects a faster pace of earnings. Reference the following equations:

Current Pace of Earnings:

$$\text{TTaM Pace} = \frac{\$1{,}000{,}000}{\$50{,}000 \text{ yearly}} = 20 \text{ years.}$$

Future Pace of Earnings:

$$\text{TTaM Pace} = \frac{\$1{,}000{,}000}{\$100{,}000 \text{ yearly}} = 10 \text{ years.}$$

As you can see from the results above, it will take 10 years to turn a million if you have an income of $100,000. If this is your goal 10 years from now, you are, in essence, planning to accelerate your pace of earnings. When you reach that goal, basically, you will be able "To Turn a Million" twice as fast.

As a visual, let's view this in the context of a number line. The tick marks between the number line reflect the incremental growth you will have between year 1 and 10. It is unrealistic to believe that there was no growth over that time period. It is also possible to achieve your 10-year aspirations sooner.

TTaM Pace Line:

Having an aspirational goal to increase your TTaM pace is the first part. The next part of the model requires you to capture how you are planning to grow at a faster-earning pace. This is the portion of planning that requires you to be laser focus. When we talk about putting your train on the tracks, what you capture here, in essence, will be the track your train will be on. This is the most difficult part because it requires a personal commitment. This is where the rubber starts to meet the road!!!!! Let's take a moment to understand the goals you aim to achieve. This is the second portion of the model.

2. The Goals You Aim To Achieve

Where you are currently is a result of a plan. That plan could have been formal or informal. Going forward; we want to develop a formal plan. A formal plan requires you to be more committed to your goals. These goals should be aspirational and beyond your current situation. Let us start by reflecting on your current situation:

- Does your current situation allow for advancement? If it does, where to? If it doesn't, why not?

- Does that advancement have incremental earning??? If so, how much???
- Do you know where you want to be next??? If the answer is yes, write the destination down.

What you are capturing is a position title if you are employed. For a business, you are documenting a segment of business you want to grow, or a new product, or service you want to supply. For example, I modeled a couple of goals so you can have insight into what is needed.

Reference the following view. Note that growth in this phase happens within levels. Level 1 can be the current condition. Levels 2 and 3 will need to be forward-looking. Higher levels reflect where you are advancing to, which is noted by the direction of the arrows shown below.

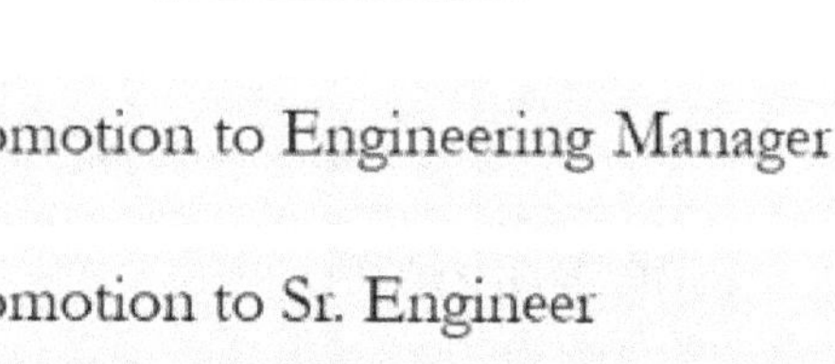

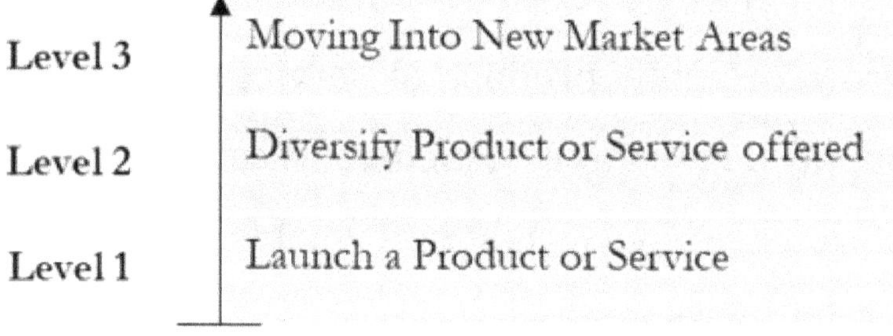

There are some ground rules with this portion of the model. First, what you document during this phase must align with your TTaM aspirations. You want to ensure your plan improves your earnings pace as you move from one level to the next. If the plan does not improve your TTaM pace, you may be only considering options that exist within your comfort zone and not pursuing breakthrough growth opportunities. If that is the case, you need to recognize that your fears may be ruling your forward progress. Remember, your wealth goals. For inspiration, go back and revisit your "why." Reconnect with your burning platform, be willing to overcome your fears, and "Think Next Step."

You can repeat this process as often as necessary to reflect the levels you need for your desired earnings. It is important to note that how long you spend at each level can determine if you are on pace to reach your goal within 10 years. That is why "Time" is the third element of the model. Let's discuss it.

3. The Timing Required For Your Goals

There is a degree of truth needed when setting the timing. It's not typical to move from one level to the next overnight. Therefore, when we decide how long it will take us to get to the next level of growth, we need to balance that perspective with some empirical norms. For a person who is planning to move from one role to the next, the person will have to understand the politics, knowledge, and experience needed to make that advancement. If the plan is for a business, there are some connections that must be made. These connections can provide the product or services additional exposure. So, let's be realistic when we set the period of time associated with where we want to be as we grow. I have found that the time in a role can be longer when a person is not willing to make the needed sacrifices that will get them to the next level. We have to be conscious of this as we execute the plan. It's also good to know the sacrifices during goal setting phase. Let's look at how time connects to the goals.

<u>Career Goals</u>   <u>Timing</u>

Level 3   Promotion to Engineering Manager   7th years

Level 2   Promotion to Sr. Engineer   4th years

Level 1   Entry Level Position - Engineering   1st years

OR

<u>Business Development Goals</u>   <u>Timing</u>

Level 3   Moving Into New Market Areas   7th years

Level 2   Diversify Product or Service offered   4th years

Level 1   Launch a Product or Service   1st years

The time at each level reflects two things. First, the timeframe informs you of the amount of time you are planning to be at your current state, as well as how long it will be before you get to the next level.

Your personal wealth plan is a dynamic model. As new factors develop during execution, it may be necessary to adjust the allotted time. If you are moving faster than you anticipated, you can reflect that within the plan. By that same token, if you are moving slower, it should be updated to reflect that as well. As time passes while you are in the role, it will serve you well to increase your skills or build the necessary connections. Through development, you will enable the growth needed for advancement to the next level, which takes us to the 4th element of the model.

4. The Personal Development Plan

To ensure we are ready for advancement to the next goal, we need to be accountable for personal development. Our approach for development will be centered on where we are with our current skills and abilities and what is needed for success at the next level. Having this insight aligns with the fundamentals of "Think Next Step." This part of the plan is so important and cannot be overlooked. This part of the plan helps us to acknowledge our areas of strengths and weaknesses so that we don't move forward when we are not ready for what lies ahead.

At times, we desire growth. But, if we receive it in advance of our readiness, there could be hardship. We want to minimize hardships as we grow. Below is a visual example of planned development. The developmental needs will change from person to person or business to business. The development we seek should align with the level of success we are pursuing and should be forward-looking.

Now that all elements of the TTaM model have been explained let's review how these 4 elements come together to form the plan. Reference the following diagrams:

A.   Career Example:

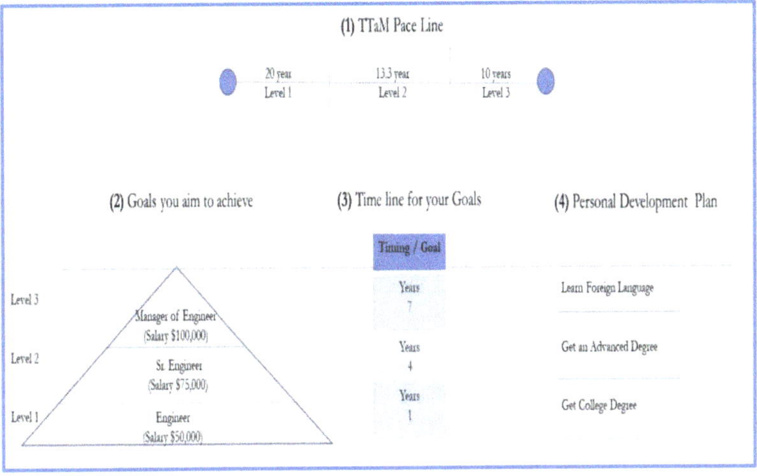

B. Business Example:

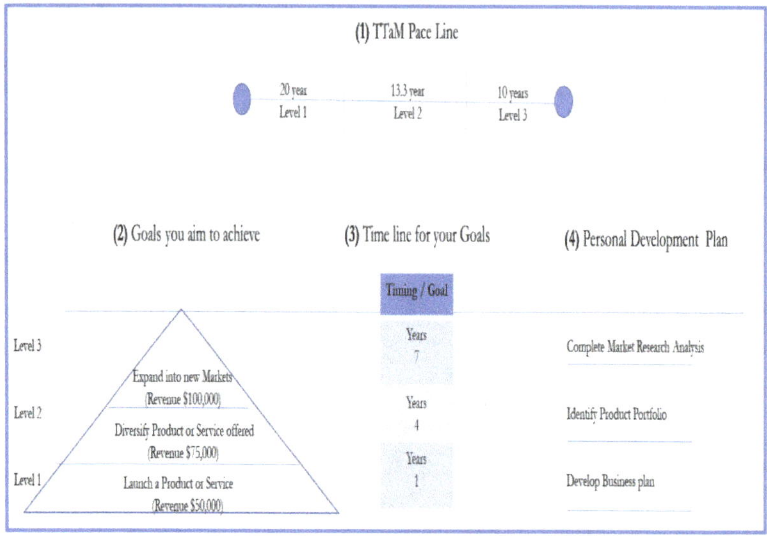

As you can see, the elements come together to form a TTaM Plan. This view is considered to be the TTaM Wealth Planning Model. The TTaM pace line forecasts incremental progress in earnings and a 10-year TTaM pace by the time level 3 is reached in year 7 of this plan. To enable growth, the development plan will align with where we are currently and what is needed for the next level. Now that we have the plan, let's understand how this plan helps with building wealth.

Chapter 5

Why TTaM?

Up to this point, we have been learning the fundamentals of TTaM, and complimented the fundamentals with reasons for why building a wealth plan is advantageous. This chapter will delve into the psychology of To Turn a Million. By now, we know our "why." Let us now focus our attention on "Why TTaM."

If you are someone who's money runs out before the end of the month, basically having more "month than money" or "more debt than income," you probably need this methodology urgently (reference diagrams below for context). If you are someone who wants to make meaningful pivots in your life but do not know how to go about it, this is a great place to start. The TTaM approach is also great for someone who is on the right track and doing well. Some folks need to have a fair amount of support to remain focused and motivated in their endeavors, as they pursue aspirational goals.

More month than Money

Money

Month

More debt than income

Income

Debt

TTaM provides a great way to combine goal attainment and income into a single strategy for long-term growth. In doing so, we are able to connect the dots for how much money a person can earn given the number of years they are planning to work. Let's bring context to this point of view. Has it ever dawned on you how much a person makes over the course of a 30-year career? Think about it for a moment. If someone makes $50,000 a year for 30 years, over the course of their career, they will earn $1.5 Million. If the person was able to increase their income to $100,000 a year within the first 10 years, their earnings would substantially accelerate to $2.5 Million earned during the course of the same time frame. Reference the illustration below.

Maxed out at $100,000

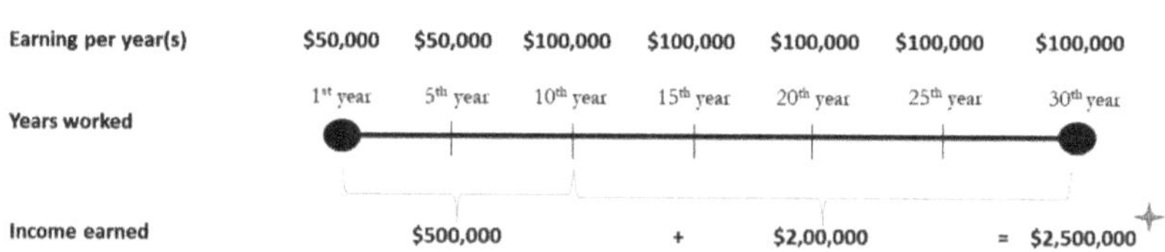

As you can see, increasing the pace of earning will provide an exponential jump in how much you will earn during the course of a career or by growing a business. Let's look at the earnings for a person who increased their income to $125,000 after 15 years of working. Reference the illustration below. In this example you can see where the model depicts someone who achieved their target earnings of $100,000 by year 10 of their career. They were then able to grow the earnings to $125,000. When you place a value on the additional $25,000 gained by increasing annual earnings to $125,000 per year, you realized it added an additional $375,000 of income for the last 15 years worked. Overall, the person will earn throughout their career $2,875,000 over the 30-years. (Compare this illustration to the previous illustrations of Maxing out at $100,000 and $125,000 for context).

Maxed out at $125,000

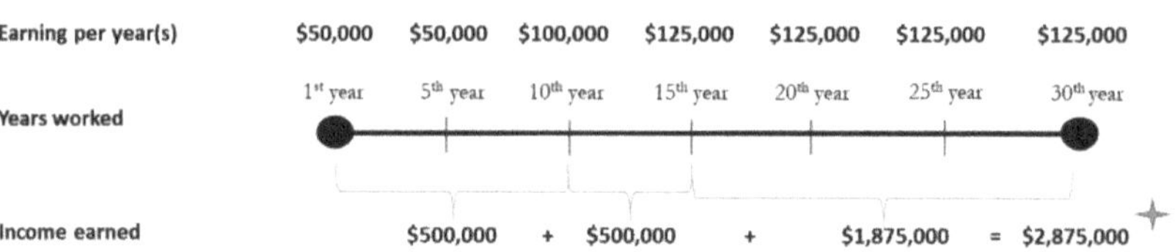

As you can see from the illustration above, by not peaking at $100,000, the incremental gain in earnings is exponential. The bigger point here ties back to building wealth. Let's explore that point.

We marvel at the potential of becoming a millionaire. The potential of it happening is very elusive. It's probably one of the reasons why we leave the possibility of achieving it to things like hitting the lottery, becoming a professional athlete, or celebrity. Achieving success in one of these areas could make you a millionaire, because the pace of earnings could be faster than normal. Now that you understand TTaM, you realize this point. The pace of earnings from these 3 potential income areas could provide the opportunity to save money. Celebrities and Athletes have been known to earn millions by simply signing a 7-figure compensation contract. Lottery winners have been known to achieve 7 figure growth overnight. However, the probability of achieving success this way is statistically low. That's why planning for wealth is so important. We can leverage earnings to help achieve it.

Let's explore how wealth is gained from the pace of earnings. The example above looks at how increasing the pace of earning creates more money earned over 30-years. We can now consider how the additional money can grow through compounding interest.

The premise here is that the amount of money you make over a given period can increase your potential to build wealth. The example above reflects earnings of $2,875,000 over a 30-year period. At this pace of earnings, you may be able to save some of the additional earnings. This portion of money can be leveraged to build wealth. What if you were able to save 10% of the money you earned during that period? For the first phase of earnings, you will save $5,000 each year for the first 10 years and then $10,000 each year for the next 20 years. With a consistent compounding interest of 10%, the amount of growth is almost unbelievable for the 30 years. Let's take a look at this from a model that represents both phases of earning:

1. The first 10 years at $5,000
2. The next 20 years at $10,000. Reference the graph below:

I used Investor.gov's* compounding calculator to model the potential gains. The results are compelling!!! After 30 years of consistently compounding interest of 10%, it was possible to model an accumulation of 7 figures. The results reflect a potential $1.3 Million in savings.

By first starting with a plan that focuses on increasing the pace of earnings, Once the plan is executed, you can eventually have money coming in fast enough to start an investment plan. Money can be put into an investment vehicle that has compounding growth. We will discuss investments in subsequent chapters. We can park this discussion here, while I share a previous conversation with one of my mentors.

One of my mentors used to ask me "What is the difference between a Chief Executive Officer (CEO) and a Janitor?" At the time, an image of the CEO came to mind, and it was a picture of someone figuratively sitting on top of the world, which I stated. He proceeded to tell me. "The difference between the two was opportunity." You see, from his point of view, he met CEOs who were not as smart as Janitors, and in some cases, he met Janitors who were smarter than some CEOs. His perspective of the gap that separated them was opportunity. After giving it some thought over the years, I came to realize the ultimate separator was the pace of earnings. If you have a CEO of a modest company making $500,000 a year, his TTaM pace will be 2-years. If you have a Janitor earning $50,000 a year, his TTaM pace will be 10 times slower than the CEOs. If the Janitor was able to increase his pace of earning to that of the CEO, does it really matter what the person's job title is???? I will let that sink in for a second. In the end, an earnings pace of 2 years affords someone the ability to build wealth. For the Janitor to get there, he will need a plan. We should also note that CEOs were not seated in that position at birth and typically achieve that level of success through long-term planning.

Let's turn our attention to some of the folks I witness growing quickly over the course of their career, and subsequently achieving a fast TTaM pace. The folks I am referring to did not remain stagnant. What was it about them? First, their hunger. They were goal-oriented. Second, their confidence. Their confidence screamed, "I can do anything." Third, their willingness to overcome challenges that were in their way. For example: If a degree was needed to advance them to their next leg of success, they pursued and obtained it. My entrepreneurial friends, if they needed to make the right contact for business expansion, they made them. Time after time, these guys were able to remove roadblocks or turn them into stepping stones and climb to the top of their pyramid. There was no challenge too great for them to overcome. Watching their achievement "in every field of human endeavor" was so inspirational! This is what we are after here. A driving force so powerful, it Wills us to the achievements we seek!

This is why TTaM starts at the foundation of building wealth. The philosophy here aims to get at the foundation, which is where it all begins for the most part. There are a lot of professionals who are able to advise you on what to do with your money. You find them on TV and the radio telling you to buy Stocks, Exchange Traded Funds, Real Estate, etc. Most people probably will make these purchases if they have the resources. Some people do it anyway when they don't really have the resources. If you want to build wealth but don't have the money, start by establishing an income stream. The reason I said "stream" is so that you visualize a consistent flow of income. You need consistency, and once you get it, hold on to it. Most wealth plans begin once you have money to invest. Consistency and pace of earnings can enable you to have the funds you need to invest.

The challenge for most is creating the situation that puts them into the position to build wealth. If you want to "Have" wealth, you need to establish a sound foundation first. A consistent flow of income is at the foundation of a TTaM plan. The flow of income has to be robust enough to support building wealth, so we start here with TTaM. The idea here is that we get to a place where money is flowing at a meaningful pace that it affords an opportunity for a sound wealth plan to be developed. That's the TTaM way. If we focus here, we will get to the root of how to excel at building wealth. Just like the high-money earners who have a great TTaM pace, we too can position ourselves for greater success.

In this chapter, I answer "Why TTaM." The best part of "To Turn a Million," is its ability to level the playing field. Even if you don't become a CEO of a corporation or a successful entrepreneur, you can still have a plan for growth by leveraging this model. I found this approach so comprehensive; I trademarked it!!!

CHAPTER 6

COMMIT TO YOUR GOAL

No matter where you are on the journey for growth, your next level of success requires a commitment from you. Decisions will have to be made. Just make them!!!! If you waffle on making commitments, your planning will have a very weak foundation. You need to empower yourself for long term sustainability, and having a lack of commitment can keep you from that. We can leverage this chapter to ensure the foundation is strong enough to be successful and sustainable.

We will start by fully committing to the goals. To do that, we need to know what it means to commit. I define it here to be a strong dedication to a cause. At this point, you know the cause you are committing to. Essentially, it is the mission to increase the pace of earnings, and overcoming obstacles that prevent you from doing that. You need to be able to identify obstacles, and spend some time putting a spotlight on them.

Let's imagine we have a White Board to display the things that are impeding progress. Below are some of the things that came to mind when I reflected on challenges people face daily. Take a moment to review them. Do any of these things apply to you?

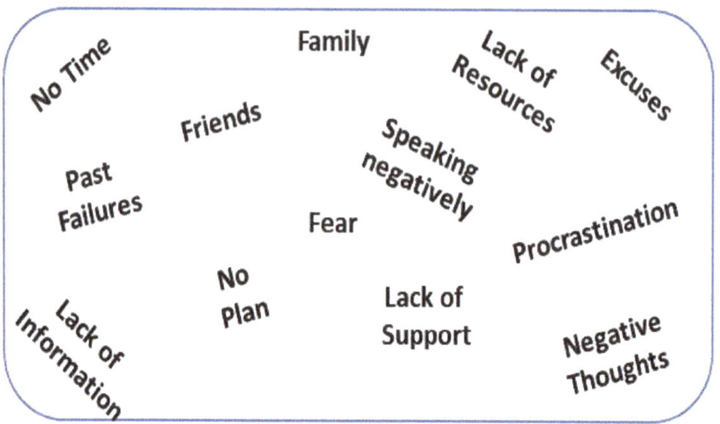

Everyone's situation is different. Therefore, I am sure there are some things that come to mind for your list that don't appear on mine. It's important to know what those things are, because we will need to unpack them. When it's time for us to move forward, these are the things that cause us to remain static.

A lot of the things listed above emanate from the way we think and the things we tell ourselves. We need to change our negative thoughts to positive ones. This is actually easier said than done. Especially when a person doesn't acknowledge this part of their fabric. It's actually easy to spot. Just listen closely and you'll find all of the; cannot, will not, not possible reflected in the things they say. They will go as far as speaking negatives about others versus being uplifting. When I come across people like that, I often feel that they have lost the ability to be positive, or the ability to continue dreaming of what is possible for their life and others. For this portion of our engagement, we are not going deep enough to address it, but to bring attention to the things that can keep you stagnant and in your comfort zone.

The diagram below reflects our personal development goals. We need to work on the things that are holding us back, and at the same time, increase the things that inspire us to do more.

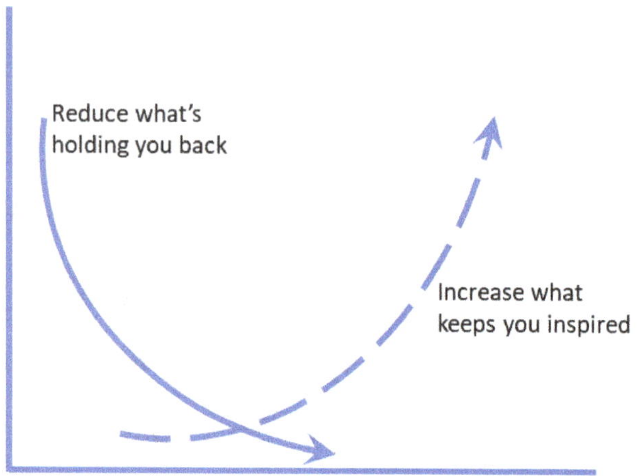

What Inspires Us:

How we think will determine how we act. Let's start by fixing the way we think. You heard it said more than once, "What the mind can conceive, it can be achieved." Sometimes it is helpful to draw inspiration from success stories you are familiar with. The personal journey of others can provide proof that success is possible. Allow their success to be encouragement. One of the success stories I reflect on happens to be about an actor who found uber success after the age of 50. Just imagine if this actor had given up on his life's goals prematurely. We wouldn't know of great movies like Driving Miss Daisy, or Shawshank Redemption. If you have seen these movies, you may have guessed that I am referring to the "Great" Morgan Freeman. Many people have not explored his background enough to gain a sense of the obstacles he faced. When you consider his journey, you find a fascinating story of a man who decided to stay in the game long enough to see the success he deserved. Could he achieve these successes in the later stage of his life if he wasn't committed to his journey? Possibly, but one thing is for sure, he was able to prevail, and the whole world was watching his success. For this reason, Morgan Freeman became one of my heroes. There are many success stories like these. But one thing is for sure, his was inspirational.

You can also draw inspiration from famous sayings and quotes. When it comes to achievement, I often reflect on this analogy; it is easier to teach a blind person to see, than it is to teach success to a person who is committed to failure. Just imagine the effort it would take to bring progress into the life of someone who is determined to go nowhere. This is next to impossible, and we should not spend too much energy on it. When we were modeling TTaM previously, I mentioned that there was no judgment in regards to the pace of earnings. I don't have that perspective for this area of focus. This area requires us to be more critical of ourselves. We need to look inward to grow our viewpoint in the positive direction.

There are several sources that have identified ways to improve on a person's viewpoint. One I found resourceful is titled "13 Ways to Become Positive Role Model for Yourself and Others" by Scott Gerber. Scott points out that you have to be someone who others want to emulate and follow at work or in personal life. Below are the 13 things a person can do to become a role model for themselves and others:

1) "Share your successes and failures," this is a model to live by

2) "Own up to your weaknesses," this transparency allows others to see that no-one is perfect

3) "Be driven by value," it's important to be clear on the value you bring

4) "Learn and adapt," this will help you continue growing over time

5) "Find ways to be helpful," be a resource for others when possible

6) "Become a volunteer," there are organizations that need help, support them

7) "Demonstrate confidence and positivity," positive people typically stay positive

8) "Prioritize health and well-being," a healthy lifestyle can bring balance to your life

9) "Set goals and celebrate them," when milestones are achieved, recognize the success

10) "Invest in personal professional development," reading and attending informative conferences can help achieve this

11) "Admit your mistake," take ownership of things that can be done better

12) "Practice self-awareness," being objective can allow you to see opportunities for improvement

13) "Empower others to grow with you," when others around you are growing, you are in an uplifting environment.

To help with identifying where you are currently with this list, I developed a diagnostic tool that will help you score your current point of view. Reference the Diagnostic Tool to score yourself. If you want to have a balanced outcome, consider having someone else score you. In doing so, you may get a non-bias point of view, and potentially honest feedback.

Diagnostic Tool for Measuring viewpoint:

	Positive View Point: Diagnostic Tool	a. Never Do it (Points: 0)	b. Seldom Do it (Points: 2)	c. Sometime Do it (Points: 4)	d. Always Do it (Points: 6)	Row Total (a+b+c+d)
1	Share your successes and failures					
2	Own up to your weaknesses					
3	Driven by value					
4	Learn and adapt to situations					
5	Find ways to be helpful					
6	Become a volunteer					
7	Demonstrate confidence and positivity					
8	Prioritize health and well-being					
9	Set goals and celebrate them					
10	Invest in personal professional development					
11	Admit your mistake					
12	Practice self-awareness:					
13	Empower others to grow with you					
	Columns Total (a+b+c+d)					Total Score

Total Score reflects how you see things: If your range is within   0-24 = moderate to negative outlook   26- 52 = Moderate to Positive outlook   (54-78 = Positive outlook)
Red Zone   Yellow Zone   Green Zone

By completing the diagnostic, you should have identified areas you can improve on. Now that you have some insight, it is good practice to decide on the areas you want to improve. It may be difficult to improve all 13 focus areas at once. It's probably best to start small. This can be done by identifying 3 to 4 areas to focus on initially. When you find growth in the initial areas, begin building on that growth by selecting the area(s) you want to work on next. The personal development areas you prioritize, should align with goals you are trying to achieve.

What's Holding Us Back:

Now that we have a perspective on how to stay inspired, there is a self-imposed roadblock that we should discuss. The road block I am referring to is called "Fear." Fear is something we face from within. It is also one of the things that drives a person to become complacent. Fear is very common, and at this point in my life, I have yet to find a person who is not afraid of something. I like to put fear into two categories. The first type of fear is driven by something a person may be going through presently in their life. This type of fear is acute and should drive immediate actions and response. The second type of fear comes from what we imagine can happen. This type of fears typically surfaces from circumstances that are not yet known, and are often described as "The fear of the unknown." Both types of fear should be confronted and not ignored when planning for the future.

There are many ways to deal with fears. Approaching fears head on is typical, but there are steps to consider with this type of approach. One of the steps is to first understand what you are afraid of, and what it is stemming from. To figure this out, you have to assess the concerns and be ready to address them at the source. In many cases, the things that worry us the most, are things that may never happen. This isn't a bad thing. When we develop plans, they are forward looking. Before executing them, we may become guarded. Being guarded is where fear is driving us to proceed with caution, and serving as a method of protection. It informs us to consider additional factors before proceeding. Having insight into where we are going, and the potential concerns to overcome are important factors for any journey.

One of the holistic approaches to conquering fear was outlined by Josh Steimle in an article published in Forbes. Josh noted that there were 14 ways to approach conquering fear. Each are reflected below:

1) "Understand fear and embrace it." Fear is the body's way of providing protection

2) "Don't just do something, stand there!" Be deliberate in your actions, plan them out

3) "Name the Fear." Identify it and acknowledge it exists

4) "Think long term." The fix should have long term benefits

5) "Educate yourself." Gain as much information about what you are afraid, rather than speculating

6) "Prepare, practice, role play." If performance is the concern, try acting it out

7) "Utilize peer pressure." Have people in your life who can challenge you to push through it

8) "Visualize success." Imagine the outcome you desire and project the goal you are striving for

9) "Gain a sense of proportion." Don't let concerns of succeeding or failure stop you

10) "Get Help." Sometimes it is good to have a support structure as you move forward

11) "Follow others, find a recipe." If someone else pioneered the journey, try following their approach

12) "Have a positive attitude." Don't give up too soon. Be persistent

13) "Be willing to pivot." If you are getting the same results try a different approach

14) "Focus on others as your motivation." Identify someone who can be inspired by your success

These are some of the ways you can approach your fears. The content within the list above can be applied when building wealth, and is general enough that it can be leveraged for a variety of scenarios whenever a person is experiencing fear or doubt.

We need to understand deeper how we deal with fear. To help with gaging this, I created a diagnostic tool. Use the Diagnostic Tool as a rubric for how fear is managed. This is another opportunity to get to know yourself.

Diagnostic Tool for conquering fear:

	Fear Diagnostic Tool	a. Never Do it (Points: 0)	b. Seldom Do it (Points: 2)	c. Sometime Do it (Points: 4)	d. Always Do it (Points: 6)	Row Total (a+b+c+d)
1	Understand fear and embrace it					
2	Don't just do something, stand there					
3	Name the Fear					
4	Think long term					
5	Educate yourself					
6	Prepare, practice, role play					
7	Utilize peer pressure					
8	Visualize success					
9	Gain a sense of proportion					
10	Get Help					
11	Follow others, find a recipe					
12	Have a positive attitude					
13	Be willing to pivot					
14	Focus on others as your motivation					
	Columns Total (a+b+c+d)					Total Score

Total Score reflects how you approach Fear: If your range is within   0-26 = Passive Red Zone   28- 54 = Moderately Direct Yellow Zone   (56-84 = Head On) Green Zone

To get a sense of where you are with respect to facing your fears, use this diagnostic tool to identify the range you fall within. The tool provides a way of identifying your current state and your approach to managing fear. Learn from it, and put emphasis on your areas of weakness and strength.

For building wealth, you need to be inspired and not afraid to do so. When a person is inspired, they have the energy required to achieve their ultimate goals. However, fear is one of the things that can reduce that energy and cause complacency. We must recognize when this situation occurs and apply the recommended techniques. When doing so, be truthful with yourself. Our lives are resulting from a pattern of behaviors. We need to find the things that are holding us back. They are lurking deep within the way we think and the way we act.

We need to stay inspired and put the right energy into the universe. We do this by accentuating the positive as we lean into forward progress. By staying inspired, we can overcome fear and self-doubt. Whenever there is self-doubt, I want you to come up with 2 reasons for why you can achieve. Write them down. Overtime, you will discover your list of "why you can achieve," will be Twice as long as your reasons for having self-doubt. It's easy to talk ourselves out of success. Going forward, we will use the techniques discussed here, to talk ourselves into success, and in doing so, we will find ourselves fully committed to our goals.

CHAPTER 7

BUILDING WEALTH

(LEVERAGING STOCK MARKET FOR GROWTH)

As we increase our pace of earnings, please be mindful of other variables that work against us. If not controlled, those variables will make it difficult to capitalize on progress. For context, if the earnings' pace increases and expenses increase equally, the net gain is zero. Here, we missed an opportunity to build wealth. As we increase the pace of inflow, we must control or decrease the pace of outflow. It is for this reason we must have a plan for wealth.

In planning for wealth, consider inflation, expenses, and taxation. These are some of the things working against our intended goal. The wealth you build must outpace them. Moreover, these negative variables become more costly over time. By outpacing the noted variables above, the wealth may eventually become generational as a result of building the commonly known "Nest Egg." A nest egg is a sum of money saved for future usage that someone can pass down from generation to generation.

An effective wealth-building plan must have the elements required to outpace inflation and other expenses. A sound plan will improve the TTaM pace and deploy a strategy for investing. With respect to investments, one may select to enter the stock market and/or the real estate sector. For diversification, it is wise to have a blend of both or what folks commonly refer to as, "multi-stream of income."

As a starting point, learn as much as possible about your investments. If you choose to invest in stocks or real estate, understand what drives the investment value up or down. Supply and demand will play a role. For example, investments increase in value when the demand is high, and the supply is low. However, on the other hand, the value of these assets will decrease in value when the supply is high, and the demand is low.

Let's pivot and take a moment to explore stock market investing.

Stock Market Investing:

In our society, the stock market is well known as a vehicle for building wealth. The daily reporting and the televised fluctuation of stock prices are exciting and captivating. If you are planning to build wealth, consider the stock market and what it has to offer. A stock market is a place where shares of companies are purchase and sold via an exchange like the NYSE or the NASDAQ. If someone is interested in owning shares in a company, the stock market is where the action is.

In 1994, the stock market was where I began putting in my extra cash. At that time, my knowledge of the stock market was suboptimal. However, I did have the luxury of working for someone who truly understood wealth and how to build it. His name was Joseph Trick. His friends and family called him Joe, and he happened to be my first boss. During the first 6 months of my career with General Motors, Joe ensured I was investing 10% of my salary in the company's

401k plan. He informed me that the savings would not seem significant when I started, but over time, it will continue to surge with compounding interest and market growth. He then shared the following perspective, "initially, you will start out with a small stick, when it becomes a medium stick, move it out of the market, and wait for a better entry."

This advice didn't make much sense then, but now, it is noticeably clear. Joe, in his own way, was telling me two things: Don't be passive with your savings, and make sure to buy low and sell high. Joe's advice was spot on. To this day, I remember those words. It has been many years sense we've worked together, and he has since made his transition, but I honor his memory by telling everyone how he inspired me to build wealth. Let's explore why Joe's advice is so key to building wealth.

Joe's First Point of View: Don't Be Passive

When I reflect on passive investment strategies, the phrase "sit it and forget it" comes to mind. This approach is one of the most notable and is usually recommended for novice investors. From my point of view, I find this to be a good strategy for long term savers, and not the best advice for someone who is interested in maximizing their wealth potential. A typical saver has a steady flow of money going into an account. The account can be interest-bearing but used to acquire shares of mutual funds, stocks, or bonds. This type of investor is usually referred to as a "long-term investor." With regards to the investment community, considering someone a long-term investor is akin to calling them a saint. I often find folks making sure that everyone knows that they are long-term investors and are very quick to look down on folks who are actively engaged with their investment accounts. Folks who consider themselves long-term investors may not align with Joe's first principle. However, we are wealth builders. Maximizing growth is an important part of our mission, just like it was for Joe, who had built a multimillion-dollar real estate portfolio before the age of forty.

It's important to note that a "sit it and forget it" strategy is not a bad approach, and a person should consult a trained professional who can help them identify a strategy that aligns with their goals and risk tolerance. Once a professional is consulted for a strategy, and money is flowing into an investment, I find that most people who "sit it and forget it," consider the job done. They transition into a leave it and don't touch it mentality and dub themselves to be "long-term investors." From my point of view, this is when learning begins. People should consider increasing their investment knowledge as much as possible when investing. A "sit it and forget it" strategy does not grant someone the permission to remain uneducated about investing and being called a long-term investor doesn't mean that you will achieve your investment goals. Investments should be closely monitored and maintained.

When investing, consider taking a common-sense approach. Common sense will help bring balance to your decision-making process. Through common sense, you'll understand that routine changes to your investments may be required, and you should challenge anyone who suggests otherwise. Think about it. There isn't any asset you own that you can ignore long-term. If you own a car, a home, a boat, or a business for instance, they will require routine maintenance. If you ignore these investments, they will lose functionality and value much faster. Consider this, if you drive a car without changing the oil, you risk damaging the engine. If the plumbing in your home is in disrepair, you risk getting mold. If you don't maintain the seals on your boat, you risk it sinking. There isn't anything of value that doesn't require routine maintenance. However, when it comes to stock market investing, one of the most recommended strategies is "sit it and forget it", which is analogous to not performing routine maintenance on your monetary asset for retirement. As a consolation for doing nothing, you are titled "Long-Term Investor." Although this title is coveted, it will not mitigate the risk an investment can suffer due to a lack of maintenance. Routine maintenance can assist with mitigating risk and can help preserve wealth as you build it. To give risk management the respect it deserves, I dedicate an entire chapter to it. Mitigating risk is the reason that Joe didn't want me to be passive with my investments.

Joe's Second Point of View: Buy Low and Sell High

Throughout my years of investing, I had some spectacular gains. When I first started investing, my buy hold strategy was iron clad. From the time Joe introduced me to the market in 1994, I excelled. The stock market between the years of 1994-2000 included the birth of internet companies like Amazon and happened to be some of the best years for investors. This period is known as the Dotcom Boom. Everything was going up, until the year 2000 came around, and the stock market took a turn for the worse. Investors saw one of the steepest declines in stock market history. At the time, I considered myself a savvy investor. In all reality, I lacked the experience needed to realize a bubble was forming in the market, and it was caused by Dotcom companies whose stocks prices were overvalued. The Dotcom Bubble eventually burst, and I watched my assets lose value. It was during this time that I reflected on Joe's advice. It became very clear what he meant by "move it out of the market and wait for a better entry."

However, I was naive back then and a proud long-term investor. I knew exactly what to do, "sit it and forget it." I had my strategy, and it compelled me to do nothing as market dynamics had changed. The market was not surging; it was collapsing. Like a good long-term investor, I did nothing as the market was falling. I painfully watched my assets deplete over a 3yrs period.

Joe's advice was now truly clear to me. A light bulb went off, realizing, if you move the assets into a less volatile position, you can protect the gains. In the end, I learned this lesson the hard way. The Dotcom Bubble Burst lasted from 2000 to 2003. My assets had dropped more than 50% by the time it was over, and I passively watched it happening.

Long-term investors are taught to hold their assets, even when they are losing value. As a long-term investor in 2003, I needed to hold on to my assets and avoid taking a 50% loss. I doubled down and held on to the depressed investment. I was in it for the "long term." The asset's value was expected to return when the market rally restarted. The rally period is known as "A Bull Market." The name is associated with the way the Bulls attack. Bulls are known to attack by moving in an upward direction.

Conversely, "A Bear Market" is what I experienced when the Dotcom bubble burst. You see, Bears are known to attack in a downward motion. In 2003, I had just lived through my first "Bear Market attack."

To support my long-term strategy, I committed to keeping the asset until the favorable bull market returned. So, I did just that. I held the fund without selling. 6 years later, the fund still hadn't returned to its original value. It never came back. That's when I realized mutual funds in your retirement account ebbs and flows with the stock market. Just because it's available in your 401k account doesn't mean it has a protected status. Between 2003 and 2008, the fund was still down more than 50%. By 2009, I had merged the assets into other investments I had started years prior. To put things into perspective, after 14 years of saving, the value of that asset was the same value it had grown to during my first 4 years of savings. By 2007, I had started taking Joe's advice. My "sit it and forget it" days were over. This is one of the reasons I avoided major losses during the Housing Bubble Burst from 2007-2009.

To gain insight into what happened in the market, from 1991-2016, reference the details outlined on the graph of the NASDAQ Composite **(from 1-6)**.

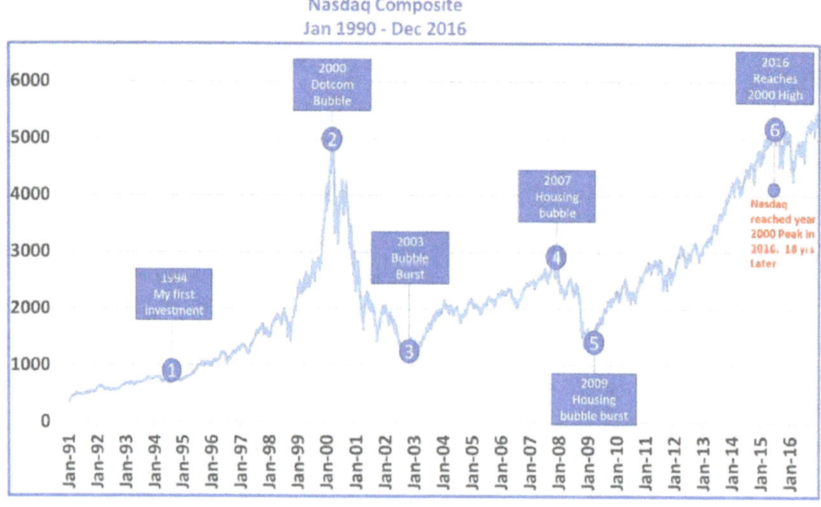

The history of my "**sit it and forget it**" strategy is reflected in the graph above, from 1994-2009. The Nasdaq eventually returned to the high it set back in March 2000. It took 16 years to eventually reach that pinnacle once again. If I hadn't merged the depressed fund into other assets in 2009, It would have potentially taken me 16yrs to get back my value. I use this example to show the potential impact of a "do-nothing" strategy. Joe's message eventually resonated with me. It took a while, but I eventually got it.

The type of market movement reflected above isn't unique to that period. Reference the graph below. Looking at 2017 to 2022, it is clear that the market continued moving higher beyond 2016.

You can also see the market decline in 2020 due to the covid pandemic. In 2021, there is a spike due to the Fed stimulating the economy by injecting liquidity. In 2022, the Fed started removing liquidity due to hyper-inflation. We experienced another bear market in 2022. If you had a "sit it and forget it" strategy in 2022, your account value might have declined back to levels reached 2 years prior as the Nasdaq fell back to 2020 levels.

I have learned a great deal since 1994, and it has been many years since the Dotcom bubble burst. At this point, the internet is now a significant part of our daily lives. It can be used to discover investment tools, videos, and applications created to help learn more about the market. You can also find countless trained professionals who are available to advise you. Make sure to take advantage of these resources as you become more engaged with your plans for wealth. In one way or another, I took advantage of these resources to expand my knowledge.

Over my years of investing, it has become quite clear that magic wands do not exist. I learned that there is no single answer for making money in the stock market. As your experience grows, you will discover a number of resources that can be leveraged to help you make an informed decision.

My decision-making starts with the following information as my investment thesis begins to develop:

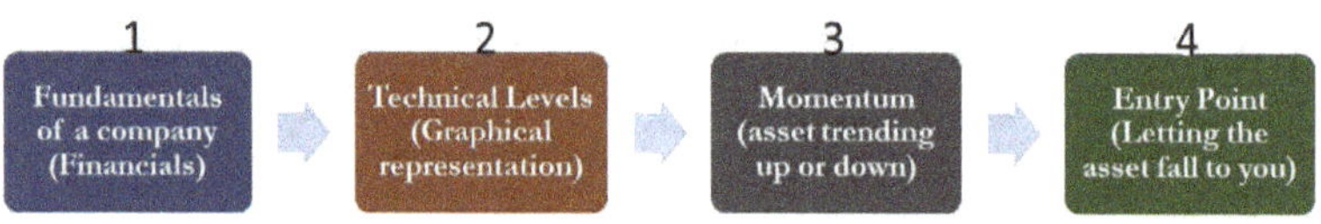

Let's review each to gain a sense of their importance.

1. Fundamentals of a company (Financials):

When I first heard the word "fundamentals," it made me think of sports. Athletes usually start developing their skills by learning the basics, often referred to as "the fundamentals." When it comes to investing, fundamentals are associated with a company's financial profile. A company's financials will let you know if they are making money.

There are several elements to look at when regarding a company's fundamentals. I like to start with the following information:

1. **Price to Earnings (P/E) ratio** – Is the stock overvalued?
2. **Beta** – Is the company more volatile than the market?
3. **Dividend** – Will a company reward ownership by giving more shares?
4. **Revenue** – How much money is generated from products and services?
5. **Year over Year Growth** – Is the company revenue growing?

6. **EBITDA** – How are **E**arnings **B**efore **I**nterest **T**axation **D**epreciation **A**mortization?

7. **Debt** – Does the company have too much debt?

8. **Cash on Hand** – Is there a surplus of total cash?

9. **Operating Cash Flow** – Is operating cash flow positive?

10. **Levered Free Cash Flow** – Is there cash left over after payments?

The list above is not exhaustive. There is a multitude of things to consider. These are just a few categories that are core to my approach. It's important to note that these fundamental areas do not limit my investment decision. As news becomes available or economic conditions change, my perspective may also change. Take a moment to review the following table. It provides an insight into the information I am seeking from these Fundamentals.

	Fundamental Profile	Insight Provided	My Considerations	Example (Data)
1	Price to Earnings (P/E) ratio	Helps with knowing if stock is overvalued	Is P/E above 18? If yes, it may be too high	6.42
2	Beta	Is the company more volatile than market	Is Beta above 1? If yes, it may be too volatile	0.65
3	Dividend	Will a company reward for ownership	Is there a dividend, if yes, is it high enough for the risk	6.49%
4	Revenue	How much money is generated from products and services	Is the revenue growing, if yes, by what percent	$155B
5	Year over Year Growth	Is the company revenue growing	Is the company revenue growing YOY, If yes, at what percent	-24%
6	EBITDA	How are Earnings Before Interest Taxation Depreciation Amortization	Is EBITDA positive, if yes, by how much	52.96B
7	Debt	Does company have too much debt	Is debt greater than 2 time EBITDA, if yes, it may be too high	152B
8	Cash on Hand	is there a surplus of total cash	Is there cash on hand, if yes, what is ratio of cash to debt	2.42B
9	Operating Cash Flow	is operating cash flow positive	Is cash flow positive, if yes, by how much	32.96B
10	Levered Free Cash Flow	Is there cash left over after payments	Is cash levered free, if yes, by how much	29.65B

Currency is in Billion = B

2. Technical Levels (Graphical representation)

Like the fundamentals, I had to learn what Technicals were and how they help with analyzing the direction of trends while attempting to predict future price movement graphically. Quickly, I realized how valuable the Technicals would be to my approach. As I reviewed the Technicals, I began learning the habit and historical movement associated with stock prices. Studying Technicals allowed me to move past daily S&P500 updates and get to know more deeply the assets I wanted to buy.

To gain a sense of how the Technicals add value, reference the details of the following chart.

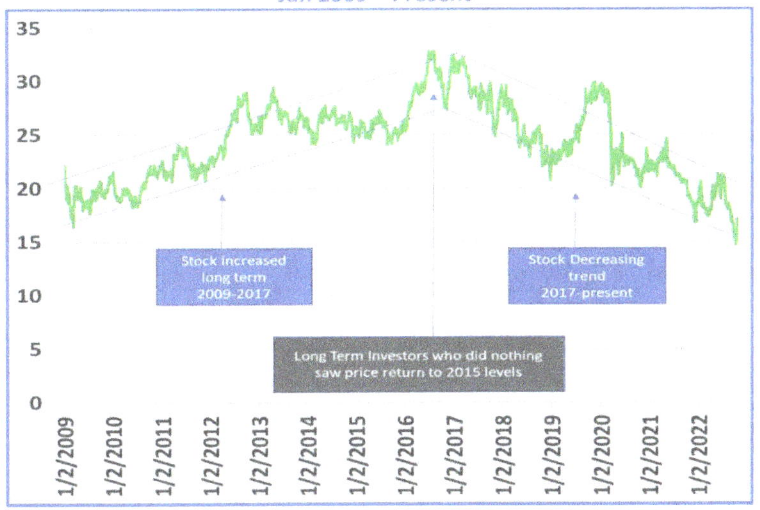

The chart represents a company that is a part of the S&P500. It provides a much closer look at the company's past performance. As you can see, from 2009, the company's stock price increased for 8 years. Eventually, there was a change in economic conditions, and the stock began to decline for the next 5 years. Those who own this stock and had a "sit it and forget it" strategy, they watched this stock reach its peak in 2016 and then decline steadily for the next 6 years. In 2022, the stock was back to 2009 levels.

A more engaged investor could have used Technicals to understand this stock's trend. The trend provides a picture of the decline in value and suggests that profits should be taken before all gains evaporate. The goal is to build wealth and keep it. The example above characterizes how I perceive long-term investors. They typically allow gains to deplete without making an adjustment.

My approach would have driven me to assess the fundamentals and the Technicals to determine if now is a good time to take profits. Two things would have guided my actions: (1) From the Fundamentals, YoY Revenue growth is negative -24%, which means the company is not growing revenue. (2) From the Technicals, the stock fails to achieve new highs and has since pivoted to a downward trend. This bit of information may be enough to consider taking profits and looking for a better purchase price in the future.

3. **Momentum (asset trending up or down)**

Once you decide the asset is worth buying, consider the momentum. Momentum speaks to the velocity (speed) at which the stock price changes. Overtime, pricing can move fast or slowly. It depends on the interest level. Every stock has a pace, no matter which direction it is moving. Using the company modeled in the example above, let's see how momentum changes. Reference the graphs below. We previously looked at the larger graph and saw the long-term trends.

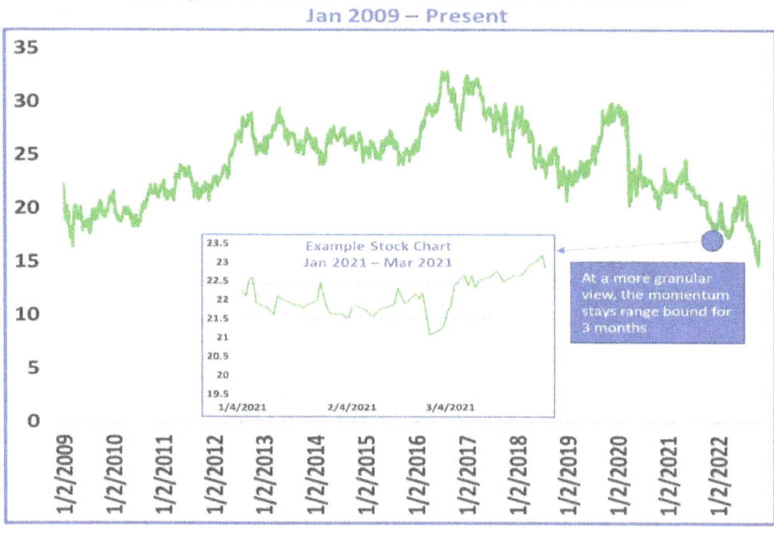

Now let's look at the smaller graph within the larger graph. The smaller graph isolates the period from Jan 2021 – March 2021. By taking a closer look at the smaller graph, you see a slightly different picture observed from the long-term data set. The long-term graph shows a decreasing trend. As you look at the movement on the smaller graph, you see the stock moved side-ways for 3 months before having a slight breakout higher in March 2021. This point of view is helpful when considering how long you will need to own an asset before capitalizing on the gains. As you see from the shorter period, even though the long-term trend is downward, there was still an opportunity to make money from this investment. As a long-term investor, I should also consider adjusting how long I hold the investment, given that the long-term trend is working against me. This is what some novices are missing. They think you are supposed to hold onto an investment no matter what. But when you consider the Fundamentals, the Technicals, and the Momentum, actions should be taken to preserve incremental gains as you build wealth.

4. Entry Point (Letting the asset fall to you)

At this point, you have a picture of the Fundamentals, the Technicals, and the Momentum. If the asset is still of interest, determine the purchase price and make a bid. This action seems simple, but this is the most important part. By executing this step, you will take ownership of company shares. If you buy too high, you can immediately see a loss of value.

For this reason, I like to let the stock price fall to a lower price before I buy it. I typically set a buy price lower than the current asking price. If I am firm on my bid price, I may have to wait awhile for the asset to eventually fall to the price I want. It could take days, weeks, months, or years for it to get to my price. Patience is a virtue as they say. This approach allows the prices to come down a fair amount. I don't want to buy at an ultimate high, hoping it will go higher from there. By buying the asset at a lower price, I increase the probability of making a profit. Buy low – Sell high has always been the name of the game. By letting the price fall to your level of interest, you will at least have room for the asset to grow back to the previous high.

Now that we have a perspective on the stock market, let's examine real estate investing.

CHAPTER 8

DIVERSIFY WEALTH

(LEVERAGING REAL ESTATE FOR GROWTH)

Investing in the stock market is one way to build wealth, but it is not the only way. All your eggs don't have to be in one basket. It is important to diversify your investment portfolio for a balanced approach to building wealth. Adding real estate to your investment strategy provides diversification. Real estate can also help manage the increasing cost of inflation, expenses, and taxation.

That is why it makes sense to consider real estate in your investment plans. The combination of stocks and real estate establishes a portfolio of assets that can ultimately help increase your net worth.

So, where does it start with real estate?

"Location! Location! Location!"

The famous mantra by Harold Samuel, is typically what you hear when someone gives advice on real estate investing. The golden rule for investing in real estate centers on the demographics. The location of the property matters, because it will determine the value and future growth. Ideally, you want to buy in the most desired location. Get to know the area where the property is located and have clear expectations regarding the projection of growth and value before purchasing the asset.

The Federal Housing Finance Agency's (FHFA) House Price Index measures the national growth rate; FHFA evaluates the average price changes in repeat real estate sales of the same property to determine the rate of growth or decline; and mortgage transactions on single-family properties are also considered when calculating the growth rate. Consider the U.S. Growth Rate on the following map provided by FHFA. As you can see, the national growth rate for the 1-year period is 18.7%.

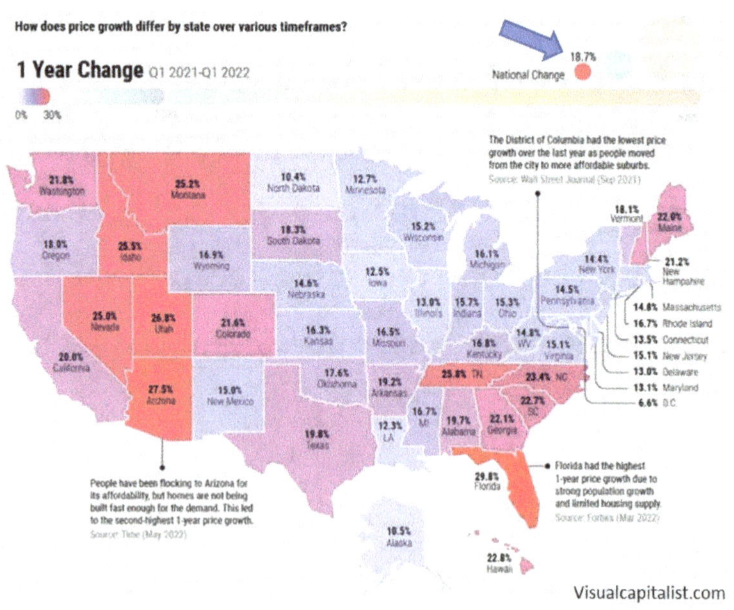

Visualcapitalist.com

The map also provides an excellent visual of where real estate growth is the highest and the lowest across the nation. As a result, one may strategically leverage the growth rate to locate the hottest real estate markets. A real estate market is considered hot when there is no shortage of buyers for available properties or simply put, there is limited housing inventory. Therefore, property sellers are best positioned to maximize profit when the real estate is located in a hot market.

The map above is a wonderful place to start for a broad view of the overall real estate economy. When investing in an area, consider evaluating the growth rate at a county level to identify the hottest locations. Local real estate information can be found on FHFA's resourceful website, "FHFA.gov." This utilitarian website contains various information that can be used to create a picture of real estate growth. Reference the FHFA HPI County Map below for an example of the information available on the FHFA's website.

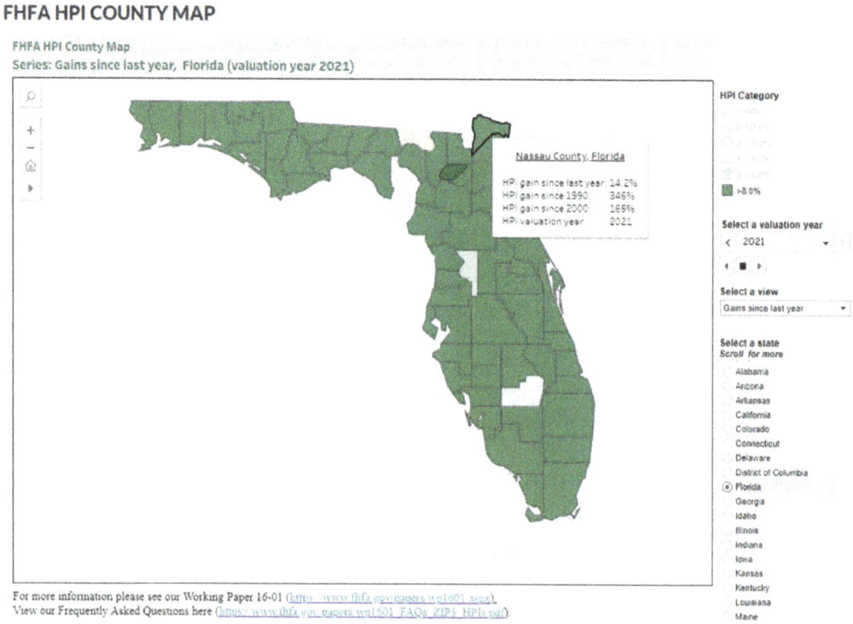

FHFA HPI COUNTY MAP

The map, noted above, highlights Nassau County Florida Housing Price Index from 1990, 2000, and 2021. Over that period of time, growth in that county has been 14.2%, 346%, and 166%, respectively.

Although the information shows an increase in the percentage, it is important to note that the real estate market growth fluctuates. From 1991 to 2022, various changes in our economy during this period influenced the price of real estate. For example, the global recession (2008-09 involved a banking crisis and a housing bubble) and the global pandemic of 2020 (SAR Covid-19 outbreak) impacted the real estate market.

Geopolitical events, financial crises, and healthcare crises, for instance, not only impacted the stock market, they directly impact the valuation of real estate. For example, in 2008, the financial crisis caused the housing prices to implode, and thereby the financial institutions tighten their lending standards.

Conversely, during the global pandemic, from 2020-2022, the base price of real estate increased by as much as 18.7% for single-family homes. There were a couple of factors contributing to this growth. First, consumers were able to work remotely. This new phenomenon led to many families purchasing property in more desirable locations. Second, during the pandemic, interest rates were extremely low, making homeownership more affordable. The combination of these two factors caused real estate prices to surge. Reference the 1-year map provided by New York Life Investments for growth across the nation during that period.

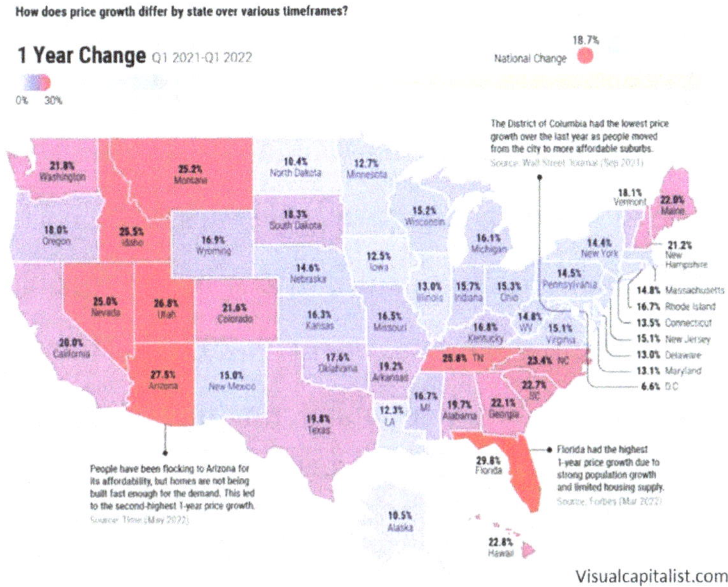

Meanwhile, when it comes to investing in real estate, the 1-year map helps with understanding the short-term view of the real estate market. It is also important to have a medium and long-term perspective as well. For a medium-term view, consider the 5-year map below. The 5-year map gives a more intermediate view of property values in locations of interest. This view is also an effective way to compare the same areas' short-term and intermediate growth rates. Suppose you compare a location such as Florida. In that case, while the rate of change over 5 years is 81.5% for the intermediate period, the rate of growth during the 1-year time frame is 29.8%. Through this comparison, we may conclude that over 30% of Florida's growth rate during the 5-year period happened in 1 year. This interesting data point makes sense, given that Florida is considered a "Hot Market." Florida's population significantly increased during the pandemic, and at the same time, there was limited housing available for the unexpected massive growth.

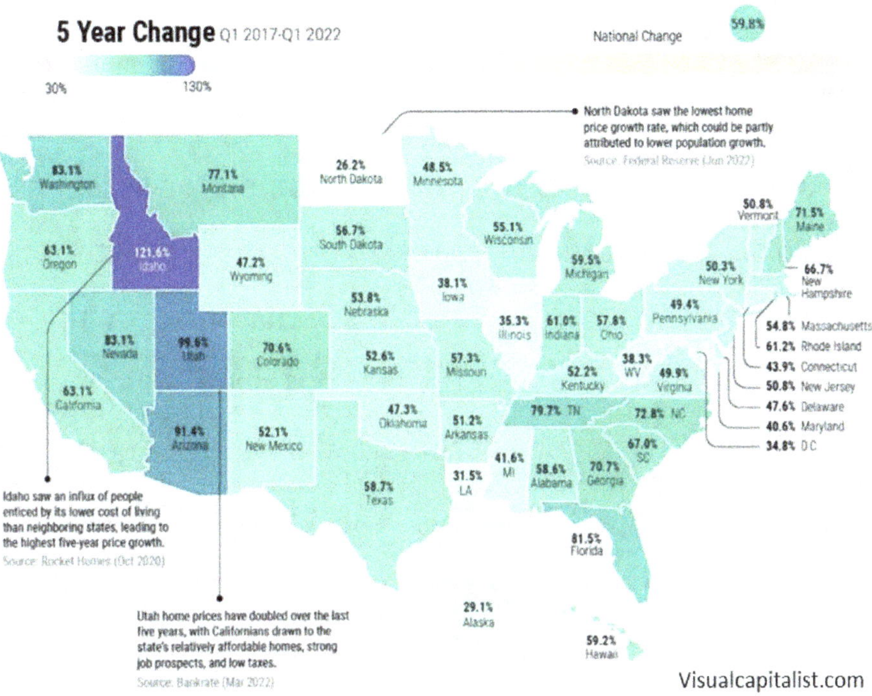
5 Year Change Q1 2017-Q1 2022
30%
130%
National Change
59.8%
North Dakota saw the lowest home price growth rate, which could be partly attributed to lower population growth.
Source: Federal Reserve (Jun 2022)
83.1% Washington
77.1% Montana
26.2% North Dakota
48.5% Minnesota
50.8% Vermont
71.5% Maine
63.1% Oregon
121.6% Idaho
47.2% Wyoming
56.7% South Dakota
55.1% Wisconsin
59.5% Michigan
50.3% New York
66.7% New Hampshire
83.1% Nevada
99.6% Utah
70.6% Colorado
53.8% Nebraska
38.1% Iowa
49.4% Pennsylvania
54.8% Massachusetts
63.1% California
52.6% Kansas
35.3% Illinois
61.0% Indiana
57.8% Ohio
61.2% Rhode Island
43.9% Connecticut
91.4% Arizona
52.1% New Mexico
47.3% Oklahoma
57.3% Missouri
52.2% Kentucky
38.3% WV
49.9% Virginia
50.8% New Jersey
47.6% Delaware
51.2% Arkansas
79.7% TN
72.8% NC
40.6% Maryland
34.8% D.C.
58.7% Texas
41.6% MI
31.5% LA
58.6% Alabama
70.7% Georgia
67.0% SC
81.5% Florida
29.1% Alaska
59.2% Hawaii
Idaho saw an influx of people enticed by its lower cost of living than neighboring states, leading to the highest five-year price growth.
Source: Rocket Homes (Oct 2020)
Utah home prices have doubled over the last five years, with Californians drawn to the state's relatively affordable homes, strong job prospects, and low taxes.
Source: Bankrate (Mar 2022)
Visualcapitalist.com

In addition to short and medium time frames, we must consider the longer-term view of real estate. Many real estate purchases are for a long-term hold. It is not uncommon for assets to be purchased and financed for 30yrs. From the 30-year map below, you can see that the growth rate in Florida over 30 years has been 389.1%. This exciting long-term growth rate is quite impressive and one of the reasons why I chose to spotlight Florida. It also confirms that adding real estate to your investment portfolio is favorable.

Although Florida is spotlighted just for context, it is important to point out other states with impressive growth rates. On the map below, there are numerous states with growth rates greater than Florida. Utah, Colorado, Montana, Oregon, Idaho, Washington, and Arizona had a higher growth rate than Florida. These locations have been among the hottest markets over the past 30 years. Folks have generated great wealth in investing in those states noted above.

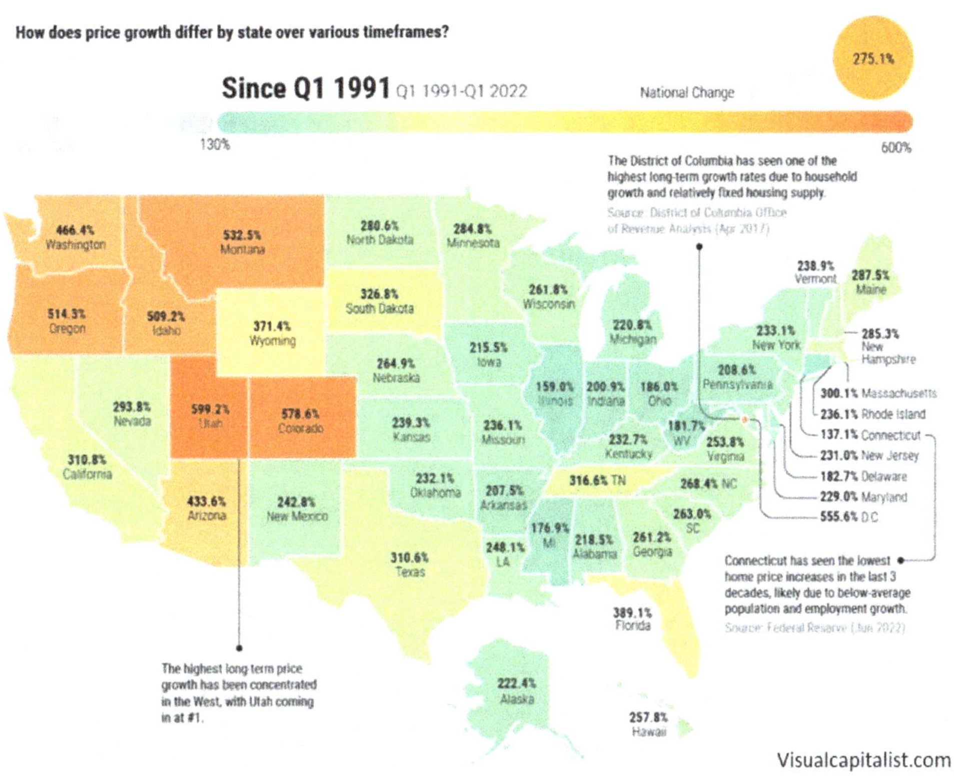

Fundamentally, when buying real estate, you are making an investment to earn money and eventually build great wealth. One may earn money via real estate by renting, selling, or leveraging the equity in the property. Therefore, it is vital that the property is situated in a location that may maximize the rental income, have a potential for a blockbuster sale, or an enormous equity position.

First, define your real estate goals at the start of your pursuit. If your goal is to buy a property for rental income, there are several ways to go about it. A person can consider buying a depressed property at a fair price and add value to it through a renovation. After repairs, the asset can be held as a rental property. A buyer can also purchase property that requires very little work at the time of purchase. In that case, the property will be available for renting immediately after taking possession of the property.

Second, sell the property after holding it for a short period of time. In that case, the purchase price will need to be low enough to allow for a profit to be made fairly quickly. By thoroughly understanding the property's market value in the area where it exists, it's possible to avoid overpaying for the asset. Before bidding on the property, know your spending limit. Putting a cap on the price you are willing to pay. This practical technique lessens the likelihood of a bidding war that results in buying a property that doesn't align with your profit zone. By staying within your profit zone, there should be enough equity for a quick profit to be realized after the short-term hold.

Several of my closest friends leverage real estate to build wealth. Over the years, I have learned a great deal from their approach. Some have even revealed a clear concise outline of their process to earn and form generational wealth. For example, reference the process that is noted below. This end-to-end process provides a sensible, practical, and thoughtful approach when considering the purchase of real estate.

Transactional Steps When Purchasing Real Estate

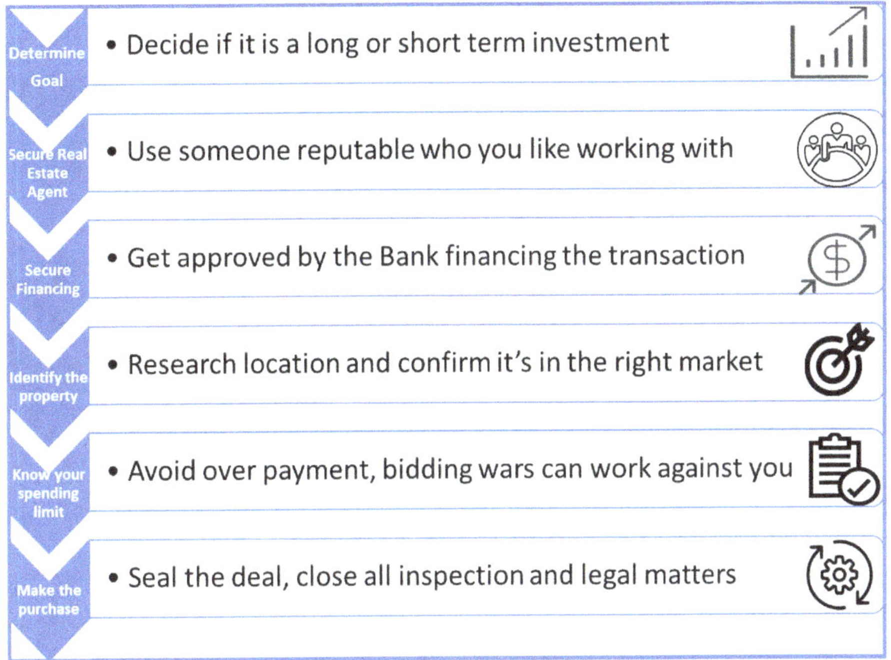

Often times, one may generate a tremendous amount of money in a real estate transaction. That is why buying and selling property is extremely attractive. Investing in real estate is not inexpensive, so please ensure that you can afford it and also avail yourself to various programs that facilitate the process to complete a real estate deal. If you are not paying with cash, a loan from a financial institution will be needed. Real estate investment is an added expense that will need to be managed. The burden of ownership is alleviated when the revenue generated by the property exceeds the reoccurring cost.

When I consider purchasing real estate, I always reflect on the advice from one of my mentors, Dr. Norman Deloach, aka "Deeno." Deeno advised against being over-extended on real estate. Essentially, "You don't want to be property-rich and cash poor." You may be overextended if your cash flow cannot absorb the real estate expense. If you are cash-poor, unexpected expenses become difficult to manage. It's important to know this golden rule before the property is purchased.

Up to now, we have mostly focused on why location and buying real estate in the right markets are so important. Let's take a moment to review the 4 conventional ways to build wealth through real estate.

Conventional Real Estate Investing

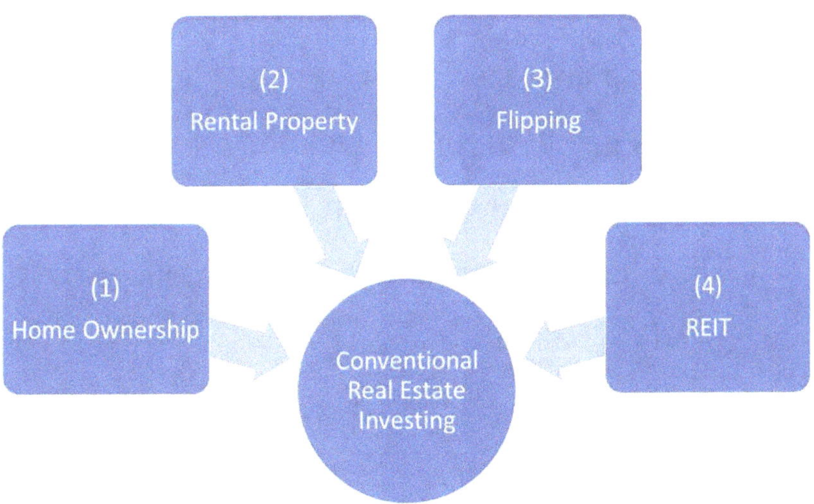

1. **<u>Home Ownership:</u>**

I hear many debates on whether a personal home should be included as an investment property. Owning a home traditionally does not generate income. As a result, many people will exclude it from the investment discussion. I like to include it. My rationale stems from the perspective of Net Worth. A personal home can be included when calculating net worth. Therefore, it is considered a component of wealth that cannot be ignored. Buying a home is a good starting point if you are just starting to build wealth. Over time, the property's market value can increase, thus allowing equity (market value minus what is owed) to be built.

2. **Rental Property:**

Rental property is attractive for multiple reasons. Like home ownership, it can be leveraged to build net worth. It also has the added benefit of cash flow. When a tenant rents property, it is with the agreement that they will make payments at a predetermined frequency and price. The money can be used to cover the cost of the property. This type of asset is considered an investment property. It is an asset that can help in offsetting inflation, expenses, and taxation.

3. **Flipping or Selling Property:**

When someone buys a property for short-term ownership and then sells it for a higher price, this is considered Flipping. Flipping real estate enables you to quickly get any invested money out of the property. It is important to get to know the market where the proper is located if the goal is to flip the property. If the property doesn't sell as quickly as planned, it can be converted to a long-term rental until a buyer comes along. In some cases, property renovations may be required. This is considered value-added work that will ultimately increase the property's value beyond the initially purchased prices. Property that is purchased for Flipping is considered an investment property. It is an asset that can help in offsetting inflation, expenses, and taxation.

4. REIT:

REITs are a terrific way to invest in commercial real estate without needing significant capital. REIT stands for Real Estate Investment Trust (REIT). It is basically a company that buys, sells, and holds a physical asset for real estate investment purposes. Depending on the company's strategy, a REIT may buy property for future sale or hold the property while collecting rent from the tenant. In this case, a tenant may be a department store, grocery store, or Doctors office. REITs are traded on the stock market. This allows someone the opportunity to invest in real estate without needing to deal with physical assets. REITs are a clever way to diversify your investment. If there is a need for cash, REITs have some advantages in that a physical property is not sold but rather shares of the REIT are sold.

These are just a few of the conventional ways to invest in real estate. As with any investment, the direction someone takes is a personal choice. For this reason, it's important to note that one approach to investing in real estate is not being judged to be better than the other.

It is important that we consider how each of the conventional options contributes to increasing the pace of earnings. As reflected below, 1 of the 4 options will not increase the pace of earnings. Home ownership can increase net worth, but it does not increase the pace of earning. The home must be sold or rented to have an influence on TTaM pace. The other 3 conventional approaches will generate income if successfully executed, and added income will increase the pace "To Turn a Million."

No	Conventional Approach	Increases Pace of Earning (Yes, No)
1	Home Ownership	No
2	Rental Property	Yes
3	Flipping or Selling Property	Yes
4	REIT	Yes

No matter what approach is considered, when investing in real estate, it's important to make sure you are buying at a price that is lower than the market value or in a real estate market where the pricing is stable and at a steadily increasing pace. Some of my friends have made careers out of buying property, renting it, or selling it after a short-term hold period. They have also been successful in owning property locally and out of state. No matter the circumstance, become an astute student of the real estate market, and your decisions will be well-informed.

No matter what avenue you take, maintenance is needed for any asset purchased. Therefore, it is without any question that one must actively engage and monitor his or her real estate holding. To make a profit, always buy an investment at the lowest price possible and sell it at the highest price possible. As you profit from your investments, consider reinvesting the profit versus spending it.

Factors in the economy matter greatly to the value of investments. It is easier to increase the value of an asset during the expansion phase of an economy. The contraction phase can bring recessionary concerns and put downward pressure on assets. It is not uncommon to see value eroding during the contraction phase. Real estate and stocks can lose value when an economy contracts. This unfortunate fluctuation is why folks must have an exit strategy.

Now that we have a perspective on investing in real estate, let's understand how to mitigate various and numerous risks.

CHAPTER 9

WEALTH PRESERVATION

(MANAGE RISK)

"The best defense is a good offense."

Achieving wealth requires a significant amount of strategic effort and consistent execution of a well-designed plan over an extended period. It's a challenging, but rewarding process that requires a lot of positive energy. Given the amount of hard work and dedication it takes to build wealth, it's essential to preserve it at all costs. In this chapter, we will delve deeper into the unique and efficient TTaM plan, which not only provides a stellar offense but also a robust defense to safeguard your wealth.

In sports, for instance, defense is about protecting your position on the field or guarding your goalpost in an effort to limit the opponent's chances of scoring. Similarly, preserving wealth (defense) is about protecting your asset value, in essence, your net worth. Net Worth is a term used to establish a picture of wealth. The net worth of a person is the outcome of the total value of your assets minus your total liabilities. (See the figure below.)

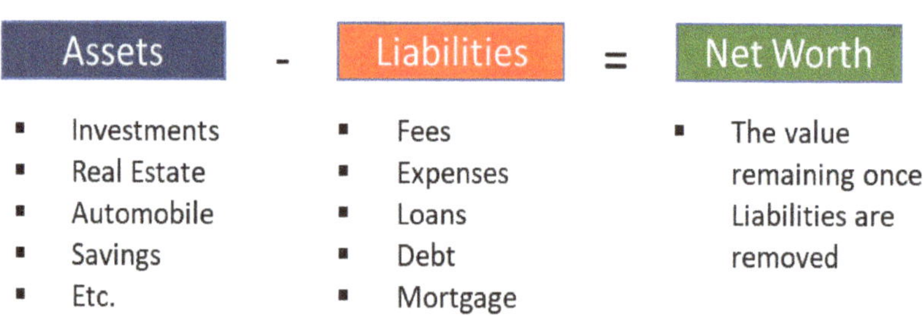

Figure: Net Worth = Assets – Liabilities.

If you have never calculated your net worth, now is an opportune time. As we improve our TTaM pace, we should also confirm that our net worth is also increasing in value. As it increases, we will continue to defend it so that the wealth is preserved. Wealth preservation is certainly viable by limiting how fast it flows out. If wealth is distributed too quickly, the net worth will decrease. Naturally, if the net worth is reduced, it is not preserved. In the end, all the hard work and heavy lifting that went into creating wealth would have been an exercise in futility.

Let's use the figure below *(creating, preserving, and growing wealth).* The figure represents a dynamic wealth creator who is pushing a huge green boulder uphill.

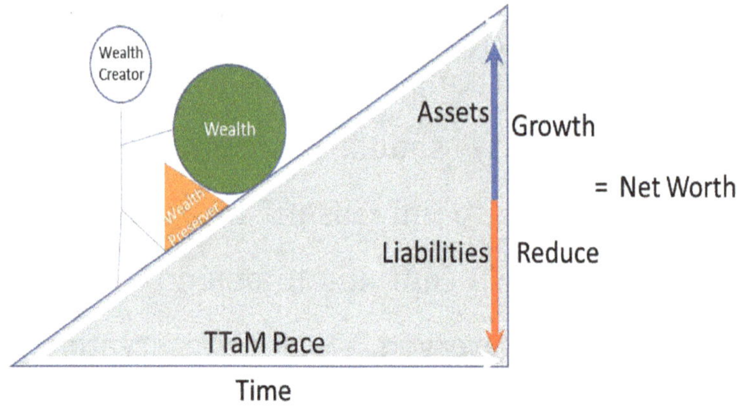

Figure: Creating, preserving, and growing wealth

This simple illustration reflects the work that is required to build wealth. Building wealth can feel like an uphill battle, but not impossible. We can see in this diagram the wealth creator has made some meaningful progress toward the goal. As a result, the wealth creator needs to defend the progress made. This defense has to be strong enough to preserve its value.

The illustration below also captures how the wealth creator's net worth is influenced by assets increasing in value while liabilities are decreasing. The TTaM pace is also reflected in the diagram to represent that it is a wealth enabler. That is why it appears at the foundation.

Studying the diagram, we don't want to overlook how the wealth creator is managing and maintaining the wealth. This aspect of the wealth creator's role is extremely critical. It is not uncommon for someone to obtain wealth and then lose it due to mismanagement. Sustaining wealth is the direct responsibility of the person who possesses it. Their job has to be performed at the highest level.

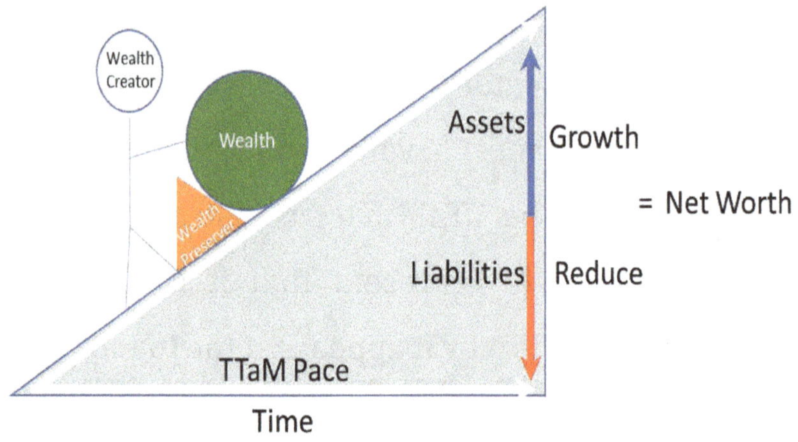

Figure: Creating, preserving, and growing wealth

As you can see above, the wealth preserver is providing a backstop for wealth by defending off the gravitational pull that wealth is experiencing as it is being pushed uphill. In essence, there is an anchored present, and it has to be forever present to minimize losses.

To better understand wealth preservation, we must look closer at the work the wealth creator is doing. From the image above, the wealth creator is clearly doing the heavy lifting. The wealth creator is playing two roles: 1. Working to increase the value of wealth (offense), and 2. Helping to preserve wealth by staying grounded (defense).

We can only imagine what the wealth creator is learning while advancing their net worth. They should be giving consideration to things we previously discussed:

1. Often revisiting their wealth plan (TTaM) to make sure they are on track,
2. Thinking next step,
3. Ensuring fears are overcome,
4. Staying inspired,
5. Ensuring investment opportunities are assessed and made, and
6. Understanding risks and mitigating them.

Mitigating risk is a skill that is developed or acquired over time. When my wealth decreased during the Dotcom era, I didn't have this skill. As I watched my net worth eroding, I kept asking myself, "why couldn't I see this coming?" Finding the answer to this question was quite challenging. The classic answer given is "just stay invested, it'll come back." What is never answered is, "when will it come back." From earlier examples, we understand that it could take many years. As a notation, all risks can't be mitigated, but we can reduce our exposure to them. I discovered numerous techniques that helped me in identifying risk(s). Let's explore them.

I think we should start with the S&P500. Just for awareness, the S&P500 is an index reflecting the leading 500 publicly traded companies. The graph of this index reflects an increasing value over time. When it drops in value, its future value typically overcomes the drop and moves to a higher value. The graph below is a good representation of this fact.

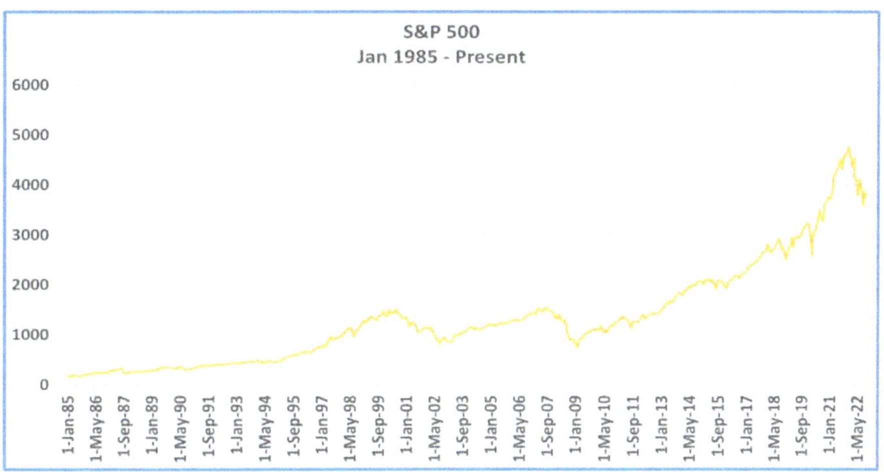

Graph: S&P500.

In order to value companies that are included in the index, the price-to-earnings ratio is commonly used. However, this method of valuation can vary from company to company, making it difficult to determine whether a company is overvalued or not. Furthermore, the degree of risk associated with overvalued conditions in the index is hard to assess. It is therefore important for investors to become familiar with resources that can help visualize these conditions.

One such resource available to investors is Schiller's PE Ratio, also known as the Cyclical Adjusted Price to Earns Ratio (CAPE). This tool provides a comparison between the current PE level and the index's historical mean. The focus is specifically on the S&P 500 index, which represents the largest 500 US publicly traded companies. By using Schiller's PE Ratio, investors can better visualize potentially overvalued conditions and make more informed investment decisions.

Graph: Schiller's PE Ratio.

When looking at the graph, I am always impressed by how far back in history it goes. The data set starts with the year 1870 up to the present times. I would imagine that we were more of an agricultural society back then, in comparison to how industrialized we are now. We can also see that the graph of the data results in a historical mean of 17. This number reflects the average value of the data set. It is possible to assume that a PE ratio higher than 17, may reflect a market that is overvalued. And could be vulnerable to losing some value as economic factors change.

Due to the volatility in the market, Schiller attempts to normalize it by using a 10-year average of earnings for the moving range that is also adjusted for inflation. As a result, we have a much smoother view of the trends. However, some micro-movement will not be so evident with this approach.

When I first heard of this metric, I wanted to understand how it could have helped me identify risk within the market. I started evaluating it based on events in history that noted a high degree of euphoria in the market prior to a deep downturn. Periods like The Great Depression of the 1930s, The Dotcom Bubble Burst of the 2000s, and The Financial Crisis of 2008. When you look at the graph, it is possible to see the deep decline that occurred during those periods. (See the graph attached below.)

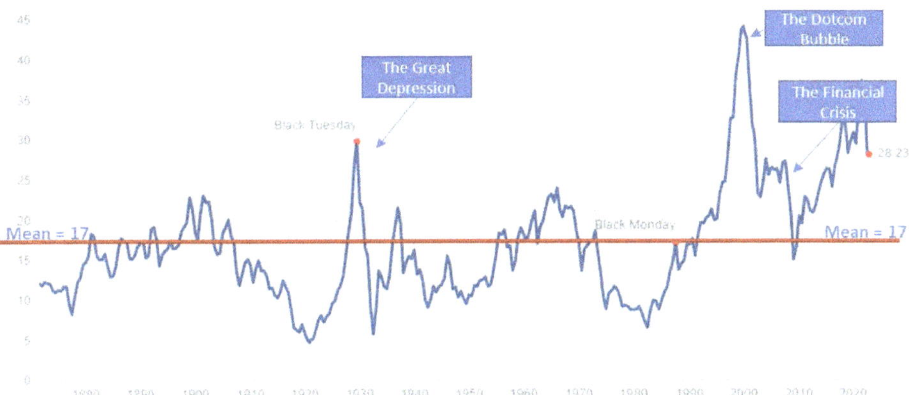

It was evident to me that the periods representing significant market events were very pronounced on the chart reflecting Shiller's approach. The period reflecting the Dotcom Bubble felt more consistent with how account values declined when we experienced losses due to that event. I decided to make a comparison between Shiller's graph and the traditional graph of the S&P 500.

In making the comparison, it is important to note that the graph of the S&P 500 is composed of the overall earnings and the forward multiple of the companies within the index. Schiller's PE Ratio (CAPE) is looking at an adjusted PE ratio of the companies included in the S&P 500. For this reason, the data set does not represent the same numerical values. However, our mission is to see the risk and mitigate it accordingly. We want to see which of the two charts identifies it best.

Let's look at the period of the Dotcom bubble burst on each chart (as given below).

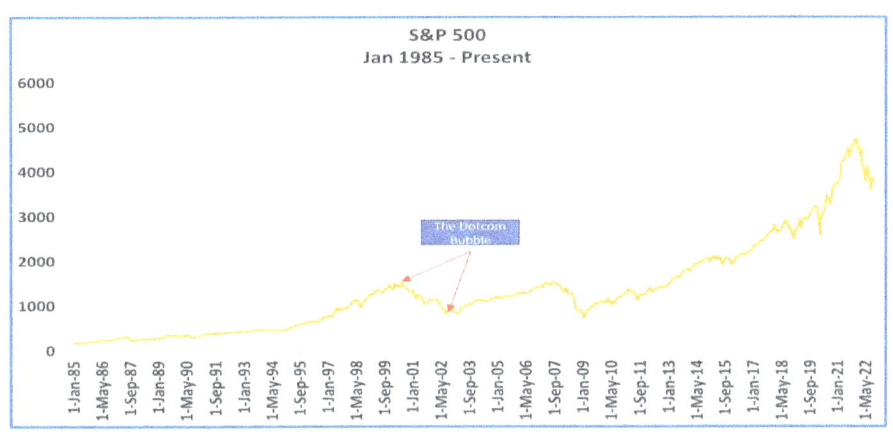

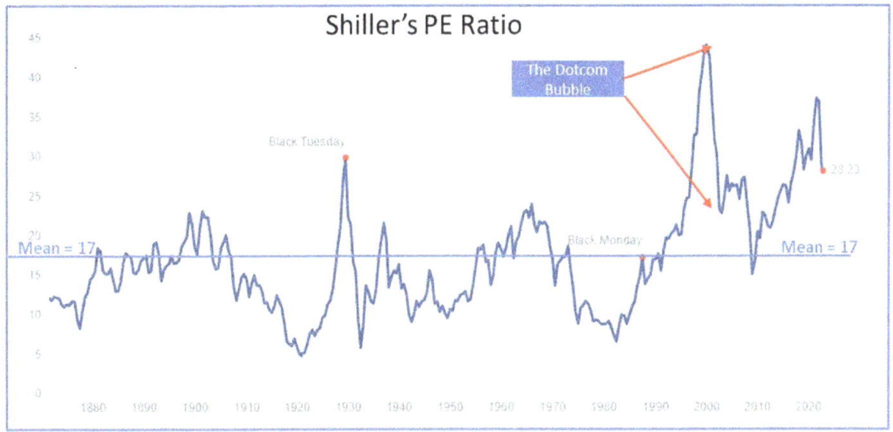

In comparing both charts, it is clear that both capture the decline that occurred during the Dotcom bubble burst. However, the traditional view of the S&P 500 reflects the decline in a more subdued visual. Whereas

Shiller's metric showed a more dramatic visual of the decline. Shiller's view reflects what the event felt like to me, and the amount of pain people may have been experiencing. Schiller's view also captures how far above the mean we had climbed prior to the fall. At that time, the only period in history when we had climbed above 30 was just before the Great Depression, and we all know what happened thereafter.

In Schiller's perspective, he points out that there are potential levels of euphoria that he terms "Irrational Exuberance." This viewpoint can be useful in visualizing the increasing risk profile that may be present in the market. The traditional S&P 500 chart also serves as a reminder that after a period of time, we can bounce back from significant declines and eventually reach higher levels.

While it is possible for the market to continue to rise, the existence of euphoria implies that risk factors are growing, and a shift in the economy could lead to a sharp decline in asset value and net worth. Therefore, it's crucial to be mindful of the potential risks and consider implementing strategies that align with one's investment goals and risk tolerance.

With this perspective, I decided to evaluate Shiller's PE Ratio and the "Set it and forget it" approach we previously discussed. To do this, I picked a point on the graph and began my theoretical set-it-and-forget-it investment. I chose to start at the very beginning, the year 1870, and pretend that I made an investment that I would set and forget for 40 years. I pick 40 years because most people start working in their 20s and typically stop working in the 60s.

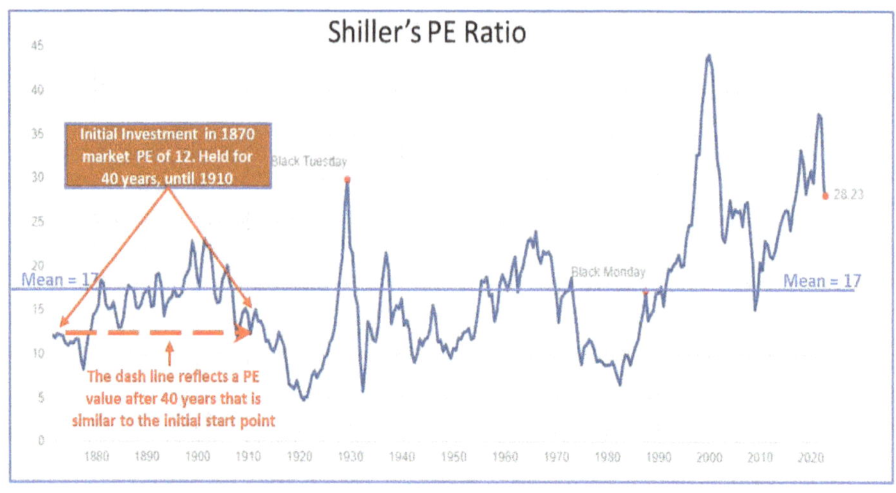

To better illustrate the concept, I use two solid lines to represent the start and stop points and added a dash line to indicate the PE Ratio from 1870 to 1910, which spans over 40 years. This period clearly shows both growth and decline, as evidenced by the upward and downward trend lines from Shiller's approach. It's important to note that if appropriate actions are not taken to protect the asset's value, it can eventually erode. As a result, one may not achieve the expected wealth accumulation for retirement, leading to a delay in retirement plans and the need to continue working beyond the scheduled retirement age.

As a wealth creator, it's crucial to understand these trends and take appropriate actions to preserve the value of the asset. This is where leveraging Schiller's PE Ratio becomes vital in identifying potential risks and overvalued conditions.

The Federal Government and its economic influence

Now that we have a perspective of Schiller's PE Ratio, we should pivot our attention to the Federal Government's role in our economy and the influence they have on wealth creation.

The Federal Government commonly referred to as "The Fed," also plays a significant role in shaping the economy, financial, and real estate markets. The Fed has a range of tools that can be used to either stimulate or slow down the economy, affecting the markets' overall performance.

The Fed's influence over the economy is akin to a shadow looming over it, and it's important to keep an eye on their actions as they can have a significant impact on wealth creation. Understanding the interplay between market trends and the Fed's actions is critical for making informed decisions that protect and preserve wealth.

When it comes to the Fed and the economy, there is this golden rule; "the Fed always wins." Whether the economy is expanding or contracting, the Fed is the antagonist or the protagonist, and sometimes both. If we are going to preserve wealth, we must be on a Fed watch.

This was clear to me as I learned more about the Dotcom era, the financial crisis, the pandemic, and control of hyperinflation. During each of these events, the Fed was involved in some facets.

The diagram below captures events that were referenced previously with graphical representation. Given the substantial and material impact these events had on the housing and financial markets, I thought it would be appropriate to understand how the Fed may have leveraged its set of tools to aid folks or to simply initiate economic change.

4 Significant Market Events

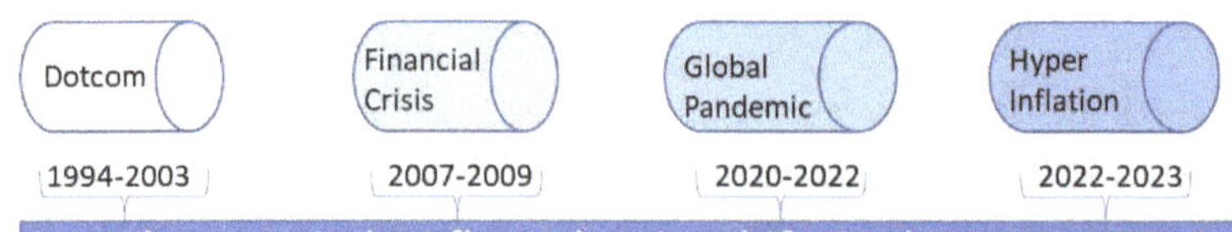

1. <u>Dotcom and the Fed:</u>

During the Dotcom boom, we saw the stock market grow significantly following the recession of the early 1990s, which drove the Fed to stimulate the economy. However, during the late '90s, the Fed needed to pivot and slow the economy down. This policy change was evident by raising interest rates. The graph below reflects a steep drop after interest rate increases were implemented.

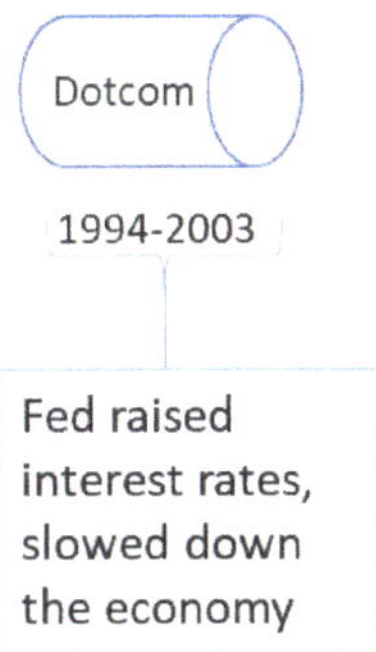

2. __Financial Crisis and the Fed:__

During the Financial Crisis, the stock market and real estate values dropped significantly. The Fed reacted quickly and began stimulating the economy by lowering interest rates to zero in 2008 and adding assets to the Fed's balance sheet. This change in policy was enough to positively move the economy. You see the results on the graph below. It is also possible to see the results of the stimulus as PE Ratios began moving upward in 2009.

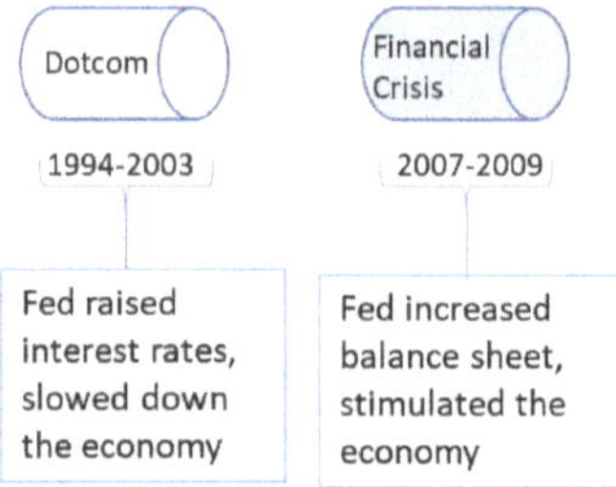

3. <u>Global Pandemic and the Fed:</u>

The global pandemic was a shock to everyone. The pace at which the market and our economy came to a standstill was extraordinary. In March 2020, we saw a quick decline in the stock market that was met by an even faster Federal Government response. The Fed lowered interest rates, added even more assets to the Fed's balance sheet, and generated stimulus money that was distributed to the American people. This policy change helped to stimulate the economy, which eventually became overheated due to the amount of stimulus money allocated to the economy. As a result, hyperinflation surfaced in the economy, as consumer prices rose exponentially. The graph below reflects the increase in market value that resulted from the Fed stimulating the economy.

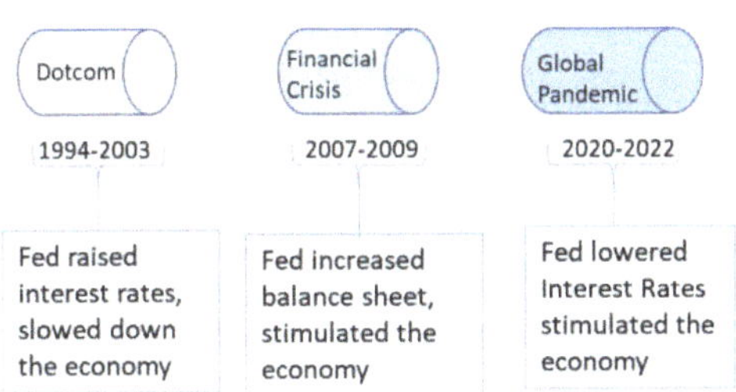

4. <u>Hyperinflation and the Fed:</u>

The inflationary pressure made it difficult for many Americans, due to higher prices of consumer goods. The Fed needed to act quickly to slow the economy. They quickly increased interest rates and began rolling assets off the Fed's balance sheet. During this period, we saw market declines as the interest rates increased several times in 2022. The graph below reflects the decreasing value the market was experiencing during that period.

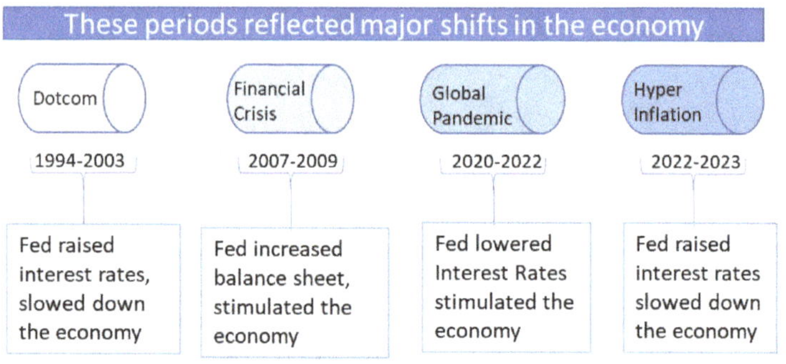

The graph can also be viewed as a cause-and-effect relationship in some respects.

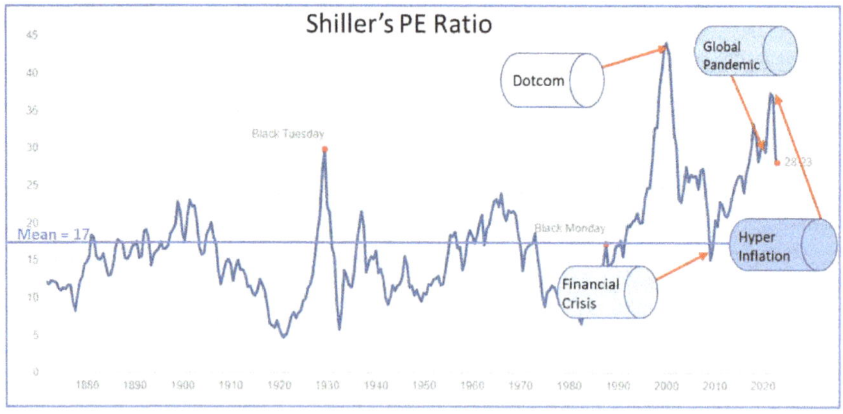

After seeing the results of the Fed's actions with regard to the markets' movement, it's easier to see why it is recommended to keep an eye on the Fed. The overlay of Shiller's PE Ratio with the Fed's actions tells a really valuable story. For the Wealth Creator, this insight when combined with other risk factors, may be enough information to consider taking some actions so that wealth is preserved.

Ultimately, the goal is to preserve wealth. To do that, we need to be mindful of the trends that are reaching euphoric risk levels and the actions of the Fed. The combination of these two factors can help when making informed decisions.

When markets are in their late stage, we typically find both of these factors at play. It may be necessary to take action by moving to a more conservative position with stocks in the market or real estate purchases. In either of these cases, once your goals are achieved, protect the asset in order to preserve the net worth that took a lot of effort to build.

Whenever factors reach a point where decisions should be made, it's always good to remember that there are trained professionals who can be consulted. It's important to do your homework in regards to identifying the right professional to work with. Nonetheless, if a professional is consulted, be mindful that no one should ever care more about an asset than the owner of the asset.

As a notation, there are many stories about people who were entrusted to manage wealth for others and ended up cheating them out of their possessions. That is why it is so important to be an active participant in the process, and guard your assets as if you are on the field defending your "goal" post from the opponent, and in the end, you will be victorious and feeling as if you had just won a national championship.

CHAPTER 10

THE CONCLUSION

Passively or intentionally, we are all trying "To Turn a Million," in one way or another. It's absolutely incumbent upon us to do so. When someone develops a skill, earns a college degree, starts a business, or joins the military, they are taking advantage of life enriching opportunities. Our society values these skills, and reward monetarily for possessing them. At the point of compensation, we start to turn a million. The pace is determined by the number of years it will take to achieve $1,000,000 of earned income.

A. TTaM Formula: For Pace of Earnings

$$\frac{\text{Constant (\$)}}{\text{Annual Income or Revenue (\$)}} = \text{Number of years it takes to earn a million dollars(yr.)}$$

B. TTaM Example:

Constant = $1,000,000/Annual Income = $100,000

$$\text{TTaM Pace} = \frac{\$1,000,000}{\$100,000 \text{ yearly}} = 10 \text{ years.}$$

C. TTaM Pace Line:

Aligns to income expectations on wealth plan.

Income at Level 1 = $50,000, Level 2 = $75,000, & Level 3 =$100,000

Anyone earning income can calculate their TTaM pace. The initial calculation provides a current state of earnings, thus making future state planning possible. The goal is to build a wealth plan that will become a reality.

Any vehicle used to advance toward a destination will have a measurable pace. For example, the speed of an automobile is measured in accordance with distance traveled and how long it takes to travel the distance. The speed influences the pace at which the destination is achieved. No matter if the speed of the vehicle is measured by miles per hour, or kilometers per hour, the pace is known. The main points here hold true for TTaM as well. It is also a vehicle that outlines timing and destination.

As a vehicle, the wealth planning model "To Turn a Million" is indispensable because it helps define and attain measurable goals. For instance, one consequential goal is to achieve a faster pace of earnings. A faster pace of earnings increases the ability to build wealth.

Origin of Wealth Planning Model

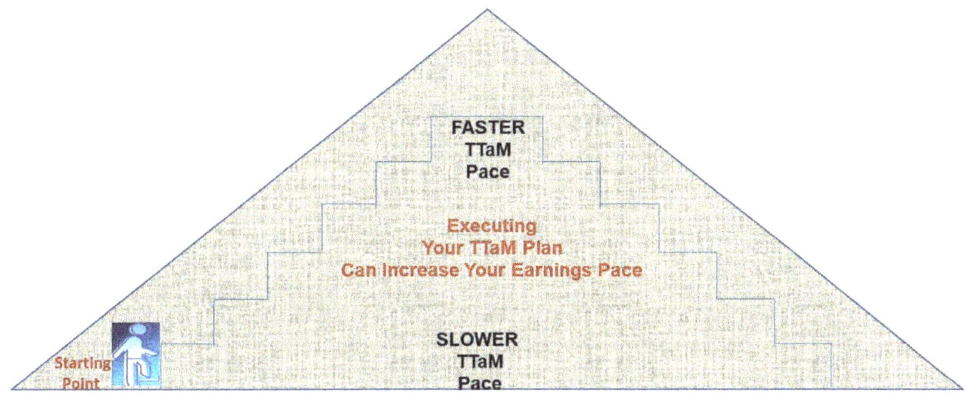

From the starting point, believe in what's achievable. Exhibit the highest degree of confidence in the ability to make goals a reality. Document your plans using the TTaM Wealth Planning Model. The plans should be realistic and aligned with your short and long-term goals. Short-term goals are micro steps advancing you toward your long-term objectives.

Dare to be brave enough to move forward and complete each area of the 4-phases within the model. Each phase represents micro steps within the plan that enables the ability to reach long-term goals.

"TTaM Wealth Planning Model (Example)

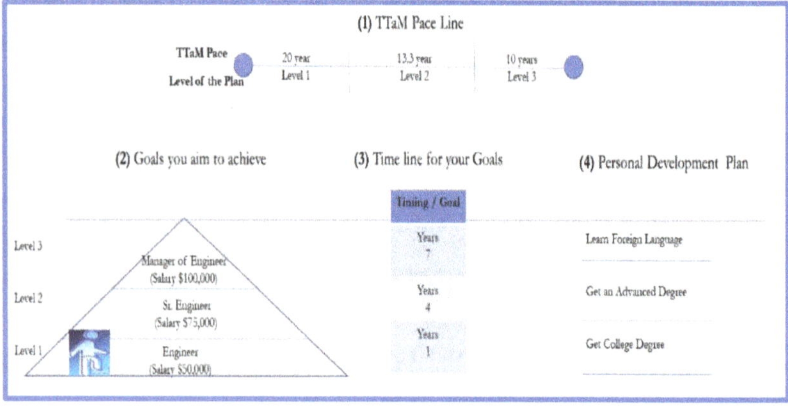

The wealth planning model is designed to get you to contemplate the next steps. Moreover, the TTaM model is an outline that serves as a guide, and the content is tailored by the user(s). Simply put, the process and destination will be personalized by the content creator.

Be disciplined and have the required audacity while executing the plan. This wonderful endeavor will require an intense focus on controllable and uncontrollable factors. We need to stop giving so much energy to things outside of our sphere of influence or control. The diagram below reflects things that are within our ability to control and the things we sometimes try to control but have limited influence over. Within the circle are the things we can control. We will move outside the circle those things we have limited control over. Depicted in red, expenses and naysayers are things that we will have limited control over but must minimize or remove their influence. In other words, if there are negative people in your life, minimize or remove the influence they have over you. You own the life you are living. Take charge of it!!!

Sphere of Influence vs. Sphere of Limited Control

When something or someone is holding us back, we need to break the chains! We cannot be afraid to address the things that keep us stagnant. Our mindset should put us in the driver's seat of the life we want to live. We can remove from the vehicle the negative elements that impact the speed and acceleration of our plans. Leaving these toxic things inside the vehicle will result in random braking and frequent stops. These occurrences definitely impact the time it takes to reach the destination. Keep those things that provide accountability, encouragement, inspiration, and motivation inside your vehicle. If you take these decisive steps, you will travel in Godspeed toward the intended goals.

After taking steps to build and initiate the plan, you move into the phase of execution. At this phase, we have the building blocks and are able to advance the plan in the right direction. Over time, momentum will increase. Use it to keep moving forward. It's ok to slow down from time to time. Just think, if you hit a bump at full speed, the vehicle will receive a higher degree of damage. The right speed allows us to read road conditions and react accordingly. Progress is still achieved by staying the course and putting in the hard work.

Progressing the Wealth Planning Model (Putting in the Work)

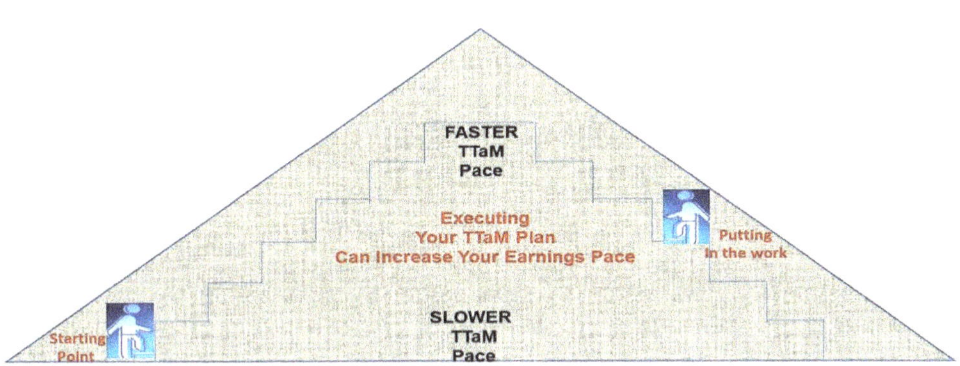

When Phases 1 through 4 of the wealth plan are completed and actions are taken to achieve what was documented, the wealth creator is making progress. If development is needed to reach the next level of the plan, execute it. This achievement will justify the reason it is possible to move to the next level. Achieving the next level of success should also result in an increased pace of earnings, as well as a new beginning. At each new level of success, execute the same fundamental aspects as before. If it's working, why change it. Keep repeating the process until you reach the goal.

Success takes time. It results from being resilient, relentless, creative, proper planning, and hard work. While achieving success, income will increase. Use the incremental income to pay down debt and start investing. Become knowledgeable about investments. This could be one of the developmental opportunities documented in phase 4 of your plan.

Find the investment vehicle that is right for you. Whether in the Stock Market or Real Estate, the investment approach should align with your interest. Don't lose focus on the ultimate goal of building wealth. Being called a "long-term investor" doesn't mean you are on the right track for building and sustaining wealth. In many cases, you might not be. The sit-it-and-forget-it philosophy can result in wealth being depleted. The graph below highlights this point.

Example Stock Chart

(Jan 2009 – Present)

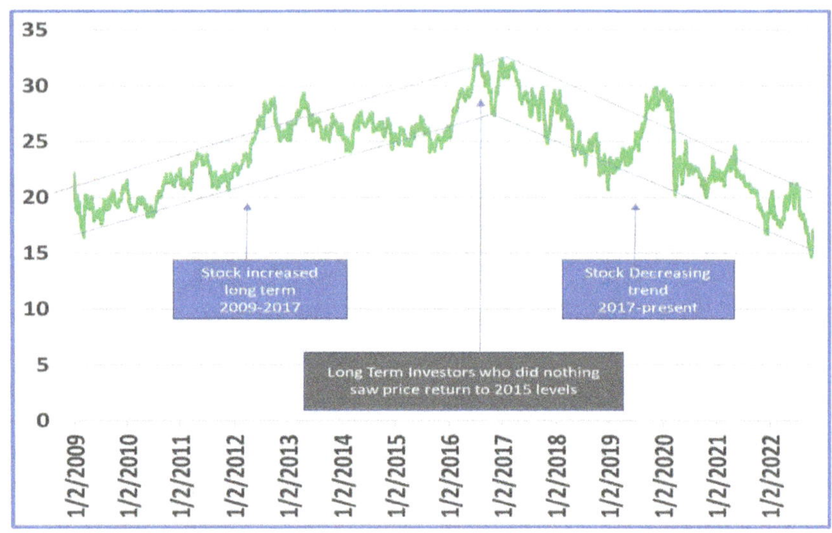

When investing, set a growth projection target. This is always good practice. While it is natural, please do not be afraid or intimidated to speak with a reliably licensed professional. Many of them offer free seminars, and it doesn't commit you to doing business with them. Besides, you should want to grow your own knowledge as much as possible. In doing so, you will be better positioned to determine the risk and benefits of an opportunity.

In addition, factors in our economy can change rapidly. Closely monitor the Federal Reserve Board (the Fed) with respect to what policies they have taken and are considering. At times, their actions signal economic change is imminent. In the visual below, we can see the Fed raising interest rates throughout 2022 and into 2023. The Fed, here, was slowing the economy.

Fed Rate Increases (Hikes)

+0.25%	+0.50%	+0.75%	+0.75%	+0.75%	+0.75%	+0.50%	+0.25%	+0.25%	+0.25%
Mar 17	May 5	Jun 16	Jul 27	Sep 21	Nov 2	Dec 14	Feb 1	Mar 2	May 2

2022   2023

In general, raising rates will not automatically trigger an economic slowdown.

However, the number of sequential times the Fed raises rates and the size of the move should be closely monitored. During the period noted above, we saw a decreasing stock market, and housing prices in some markets came down.

When you go to the bank to borrow money, the cost of borrowing money is pegged to the interest rate. For example, if you are borrowing money for Real Estate, the mortgage cost is higher if interest rates are high. Higher cost also means the buyer may need to scale down the purchase. As interest rates decrease, buyers may be able to afford more property.

When the Fed is raising rates, there can be an increase in investment risks. Appropriate actions should be taken to mitigate risk and protect asset value. Protecting asset value is an important step in preserving wealth. It is incumbent on the Wealth Creator to preserve wealth. If wealth decreases, so can the overall Net Worth.

Wealth Creator Advancing and Protecting Wealth: Preserving Net Worth

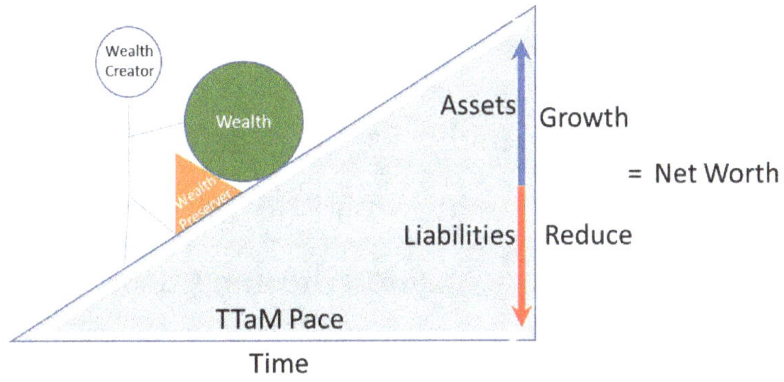

The **Wealth Creator's** role starts at the foundation of the TTaM wealth planning model. No matter if the wealth is inherited or earned. The starting point is the same. What differs is the current state of wealth. When wealth is inherited, it is sometimes gone over the course of 1 or 2 generations. For wealth to be preserved, there must be a long-term plan. To Turn a Million Wealth Planning Model helps outline a long-term plan. Within the plan, the inheritor or the earner who generated the wealth assumes the role of the Wealth Creator, and their goal will be to build and protect their assets and net worth.

There are many ways to define success. Achieving a personalized TTaM plan is one of them. When you consider the long-term goals that take years to accomplish, it is very gratifying to know that what was aimed for actually came to fruition. With every new achievement, personal growth occurs.

It's not about where you start in life, it's about the journey and how you finish. We have the ability to choose who we want to be and what we want to achieve. Challenge yourself to become the person you want to become, and imagine having an opportunity to look at life from the top of your wealth plan. Visualizing your goals is the starting point.

Achieving The Wealth Planning Model

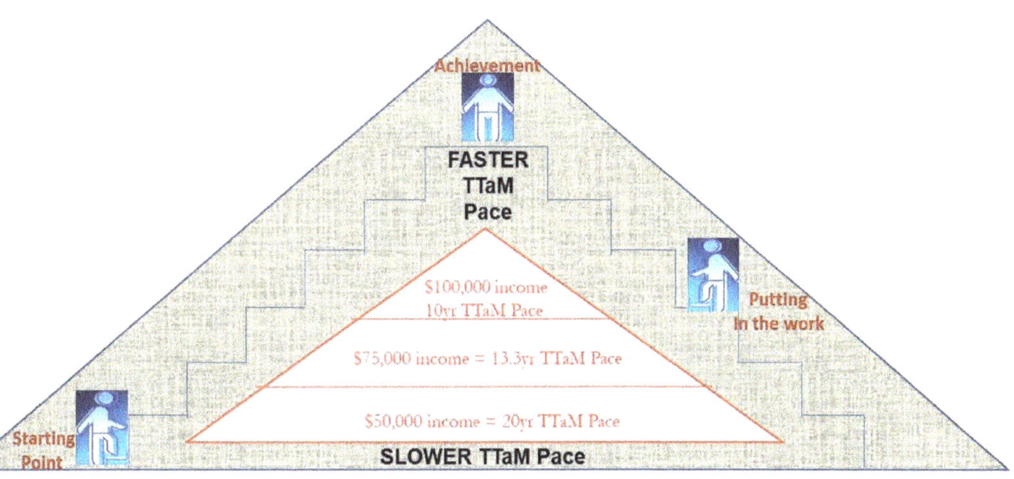

When you reach the very top of the plan, it is time to start a new plan. The peak of your plan will become the foundation of the new plan. The reimagination starts all over again. There are no limits on the number of plans you create. The plan can look ahead 30 years just as well as 10 years. It can have 10 levels, just the same as 3 levels. It can have a starting annual income of $1,000,000, just as well as $20,000. The plan is tailored to meet your needs.

In closing, I want to thank you for taking the time to learn how "To Turn a Million." I hope this approach becomes the vehicle that puts you in the driver's seat for success and wealth.

Conclusively, I will leave you with this quote from Zig Ziglar. "If you are not willing to learn, no one can help you. If you are determined to learn, no one can stop you."

"Now... Let's Go... To Turn a Million!"

APPENDIX A

To build your plan, scan the QR Code to

Download the TTAM App from

Apple or Google Play Store

APPENDIX B

"To Turn a Million"

Wealth Planning Model

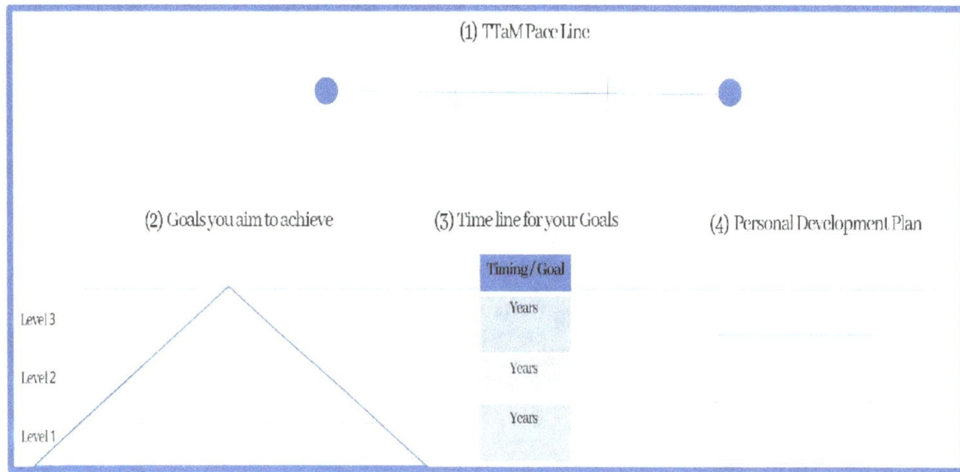